DOS Commands by Function

Function	Command to Use
Defragment files	DEFRAG
Delete a file	DEL, ERASE
Display a disk-drive letter	TRUENAME
Display information about RAM	MEM
Display the contents of a file	TYPE
Display the disk volume label	VOL
Display the DOS version number	VER
Display the subdirectory structure	TREE
Edit ASCII files	EDIT
Edit DOS line commands	DOSKEY
Edit executable files	DEBUG
Erase a file	DEL, ERASE
Erase an entire disk or directory	DELTREE
Find a character string in a file	FIND
Find files in other subdirectories	APPEND, PATH
Format a blank disk	FORMAT
Get help with DOS	DOSHELP, HELP, /?
Install a foreign character set	CHCP, COUNTRY, KEYB, MODE, NLSFUNC, SELECT
Install DOS on hard or floppy disk	FORMAT, SETUP, SYS
List files on a disk or subdirectory	DIR
Load a secondary command processor	COMMAND
Load DOS in High Memory Area	DOS
Load programs in memory	DEVICE, DEVICEHIGH, INSTALL, LH, LOADHIGH
Move files to a different subdirectory	MOVE
Pause screen scrolling	MORE

Computer users are not all alike.
Neither are SYBEX books.

We know our customers have a variety of needs. They've told us so. And because we've listened, we've developed several distinct types of books to meet the needs of each of our customers. What are you looking for in computer help?

If you're looking for the basics, try the **ABC's** series. For a more visual approach, select full-color **Quick & Easy** books.

Running Start books are two books in one: a fast-paced tutorial, followed by a command reference.

Mastering and **Understanding** titles offer you a step-by-step introduction, plus an in-depth examination of intermediate-level features, to use as you progress.

Our **Up & Running** series is designed for computer-literate consumers who want a no-nonsense overview of new programs. Just 20 basic lessons, and you're on your way.

SYBEX **Encyclopedias, Desktop References,** and **A to Z** books provide a *comprehensive reference* and explanation of all of the commands, features, and functions of the subject software.

Sometimes a subject requires a special treatment that our standard series don't provide. So you'll find we have titles like **Advanced Techniques, Handbooks, Tips & Tricks,** and others that are specifically tailored to satisfy a unique need.

You'll find SYBEX publishes a variety of books on every popular software package. Looking for computer help? Help Yourself to SYBEX.

For a complete catalog of our publications:

SYBEX Inc.
2021 Challenger Drive, Alameda, CA 94501
Tel: (510) 523-8233/(800) 227-2346 Telex: 336311
Fax: (510) 523-2373

SYBEX is committed to using natural resources wisely to preserve and improve our environment. This is why we have been printing the text of books like this one on recycled paper since 1982.

This year our use of recycled paper will result in the saving of more than 15,300 trees. We will lower air pollution effluents by 54,000 pounds, save 6,300,000 gallons of water, and reduce landfill by 2,700 cubic yards.

In choosing a SYBEX book you are not only making a choice for the best in skills and information, you are also choosing to enhance the quality of life for all of us.

DOS 6
Instant Reference

The SYBEX Instant Reference Series

Instant References are available on these topics:

AutoCAD Release 11

AutoCAD Release 12

CorelDRAW 3

dBASE

dBASE IV 1.1 Programmer's

dBASE IV 1.1 User's

DESQview

DOS

DOS 5

Excel 4 for Windows

Harvard Graphics 3

Harvard Graphics
for Windows

Lotus 1-2-3 Release 2.3 &
2.4 for DOS

Lotus 1-2-3 for Windows

Macintosh Software

Microsoft Access

Norton Desktop for DOS

Norton Desktop for
Windows 2.0

Norton Utilities 6

PageMaker 4.0
for the Macintosh

Paradox 3.5 User's

Paradox 4 Programmer's

Paradox 4 User's

PC Tools 7.1

Quattro Pro for Windows

Windows 3.1

Word for Windows,
Version 2.0

WordPerfect 5

WordPerfect 5.1 for DOS

WordPerfect 5.1 for Windows

DOS® 6
Instant Reference

Robert M. Thomas

SYBEX®

San Francisco • Paris • Düsseldorf • Soest

Acquisitions Editor: Dianne King
Developmental Editor: Gary Masters
Editor: David Krassner
Technical Editor: Lonnie Moseley
Book Designer: Ingrid Owen
Screen Graphics: Cuong Le
Page Layout and Typesetting: Len Gilbert
Proofreader/Production Assistant: Kristin Amlie
Cover Designer: Archer Design

Library of Congress Card Number: 93-83502
ISBN: 0-7821-1235-8

Manufactured in the United States of America
10 9 8 7 6 5 4 3 2 1

In memory of my father-in-law,
Robert E. Thomas

Acknowledgments

Many thanks to David Krassner for his great work editing the original, unrefined manuscript into a coherent, consistent whole. I am also grateful to Lonnie Moseley for her technical review.

Thanks as well to the following people at Sybex, who made contributions and to whom this book, in one way or another, owes its existence: Dianne King, Acquisitions Editor; Barbara Gordon, Managing Editor; Cuong Le, screen graphics; Ingrid Owen, design and paste-up; Len Gilbert, typesetter; and Kristin Amlie, proofreader.

Also, many thanks to Microsoft Corporation for generously supplying beta versions of the software.

A bit closer to home, I would like to add my appreciation for my beloved wife, Krista, for her infinite kindness and patience. Finally, as always, thanks to Roscoe and Elaine, for their eternal lightness of heart.

B.T.

Table of Contents

Part Three

The DOS Shell
29

Part Four

DOS Commands
55

Appendix A

CONFIG.SYS Commands
195

Appendix B

Using Batch Files
223

Appendix C

DOS 6 Device Driver Files
247

Appendix D

General DOS Error Messages

Index

Introduction

DOS 6 Instant Reference is intended for all everyday users of IBM and compatible desktop computers who would like an easy-to-use, practical reference to the productivity tools included in the DOS operating system. Whether you are a novice or experienced user, you will find this book to be a handy source of essential information about the DOS commands. This book also includes basic information on configuring and optimizing your system, plus information on speeding up and simplifying your day-to-day operations using batch files and the new DOS shell. Throughout the book you will find helpful tips on safer and more effective disk file management.

ABOUT DOS VERSION 6

Version 6 adds a number of important new features that will make DOS more useful and productive for all users, regardless of their level of experience. New DOS 6 features include:

- DoubleSpace, a file compression utility that increases the storage capacity of your hard disk.

- Memory Maker, a configuration utility that analyzes your system and automatically writes the CONFIG.SYS and AUTOEXEC.BAT files to maximize your system's resources.

- Support for multiple system configurations, selectable from a custom menu at startup time.

- Defrag, a file defragmentation utility that arranges files in contiguous sectors on your hard disk, for speedier access.

- Anti-virus software for both DOS and Windows, to protect your data from viruses.

- High-speed backup utilities for both DOS and Windows.

- An expanded Help command.

- Power, a power-conservation utility for extending battery life on laptop and portable computers.

- Interactive batch files, by means of the new CHOICE command.

HOW THIS BOOK IS ORGANIZED

This book covers all commands for DOS 6, with special emphasis on the new features found in the latest version of the program, and is structured as follows:

Part One: General Rules for Using DOS provides a brief summary of the common conventions and procedures you need to know to run DOS.

Part Two: Installing and Configuring DOS 6 gives an overview of the new DOS 6 configuration features and options to help you make the most of your system.

Part Three: The DOS Shell summarizes the unique features of the DOS 6 graphic user interface.

Part Four: DOS Commands is an alphabetical listing of all the commands found in DOS; under the heading for each command you will find the following information:

- Each command entry begins with such basic information as whether the command is external or internal, whether it is terminate-and-stay-resident, whether the command will erase or overwrite data, as well as a brief description of the purpose of the command.

- Syntax lines are given to show how a particular command should be entered at the DOS prompt.

- Practical examples demonstrate proper usage of the command.

- Where applicable, Errorlevel codes and their corresponding meanings are given.

- The "Notes" section that appears near the end of some of the command entries gives special information, warnings, and tips for proper usage of the DOS command under discussion.

- Many command entries end with a reference list of commands that serve similar or related purposes.

The four appendices cover CONFIG.SYS commands, batch files, device driver files, and general DOS error messages.

CONVENTIONS USED IN THIS BOOK

Here is a brief description of the symbols that may appear at the beginning of each command entry:

Note	Meaning
E	The command is an external DOS command.
I	The command is an internal DOS command.
NEW	This command is new to DOS 6.
TSR	The command is a terminate-and-stay-resident command.
!	The command can erase or overwrite your files, so use with extreme care.

The command syntax lines used in this book employ the following conventions:

- DOS commands appear in UPPERCASE letters and are followed by a general description of applicable parameters, in the order they must be entered.

- Required parameters and placeholders appear in standard lowercase type.

- Optional placeholders appear in *italics*. For example, if *file(s)* shows up in a syntax line, the actual name or names of a file or group of files must be entered.

- The presence of optional command switches is indicated by /*switches*. If a command allows more than one command switch, they may be combined on the same command line unless otherwise stated.

- All external DOS commands may be preceded by a drive letter and/or subdirectory path indicating the location of the command file on disk. For the sake of simplicity, the examples in this book assume that the subdirectory containing DOS command files is the currently logged subdirectory or that the subdirectory is part of the operating system's search path.

For example, this is the syntax line for the XCOPY command:

XCOPY *source:\path*file(s) *target:\path\file(s) /switches*

According to the example, XCOPY requires you to provide the names of source files, and you may optionally provide target files as well. You may include a drive and directory path for source and target files. Optional command switches can be included, but are not necessary to run XCOPY.

HOW TO USE THIS BOOK

Novice users should begin by reading *Part One: General Rules for Using DOS*. Some experienced users may also find it helpful to review the information in that section. Thereafter, you may use the book on an as-needed basis to learn the basics of all the commands or just brush up on the features of more familiar commands. Keep the book handy while you work with your computer in case you encounter a strange message or other problem using a command. The aim of this book is to make you more productive and give you the knowledge you need to manipulate your data files with confidence, ease, and safety.

Part One

General Rules for Using DOS

The following section describes some of the fundamental concepts that apply to DOS commands and the operating system in general.

ENTERING COMMANDS

Enter DOS commands at the DOS *system prompt*, which is usually a letter on the screen that corresponds to the currently active disk drive. DOS commands are invoked by entering the command *name;* for example, COPY, DIR, or RENAME. Often you may include a number of command *parameters* after the command name. DOS commands and parameters are described in detail in *Part Four*.

The maximum length of a DOS command, including any optional parameters, is 127 characters.

Alternatively, you can enter commands using the *DOS shell*, a graphic user interface for the operating system. For details, refer to *Part Three*.

EXTERNAL COMMANDS

DOS has two types of commands: *external* and *internal*. External commands are actually small, separate utility programs that accompany the operating system and expand its usefulness. If you are using DOS on a floppy-disk system, you will need to insert the DOS diskette containing these programs into your computer's floppy drive before you invoke them.

If you are using DOS on a system with a hard disk, the recommended procedure is to copy all the external program files you intend to use onto a separate subdirectory, such as C:\DOS, and to include this subdirectory name as part of the PATH statement in your AUTOEXEC.BAT. If you are unfamiliar with these terms, refer to the PATH entry in *Part Four*.

If it's necessary to run a DOS external command, you may precede all external commands with a drive letter or subdirectory path name to indicate the location of the program file. For example:

A:XCOPY A: B:

will run the external XCOPY command if the XCOPY command file is on drive A.

C:\DOS\XCOPY A: B:

will run the same command if the XCOPY command file is in the \DOS subdirectory of drive C.

If the DOS directory is part of the system's PATH statement, or if you are currently logged onto the subdirectory where the XCOPY command file resides, you may omit the drive address and command path. For instance:

XCOPY A: B:

will run the command under these circumstances. For clarity, the command examples in this book are based on the assumption that you have included your DOS subdirectory in your path statement, or are running DOS from the default drive or subdirectory.

INTERNAL COMMANDS

DOS internal commands are always available to the operator, and may be entered from any DOS prompt. For example:

DIR /P

is an internal command that will execute at any time.

COMMAND HELP

All DOS commands accept a special question mark option (/?) on the command line. When a command name is followed by this option, DOS does not execute the command, but instead displays a terse description of the particular command's syntax and usage. For example:

    COPY /?

returns the following:

    Copies one or more files to another location.

    COPY [/A | /B] source [/A | /B] [+ source [/A | /B] [+ ...]]
    [destination [/A | /B]] [/V]

      source   Specifies the file or files to be copied.

      /A   Indicates an ASCII text file.

      /B   Indicates a binary file.

      destination   Specifies the directory and/or filename for the
      new file(s).

      /V   Verifies that new files are written correctly.

    To append files, specify a single file for destination, but
    multiple files for source (using wildcards or file1+file2+file3
    format).

FUNCTION KEYS

DOS provides a limited but handy set of special function keys that assist you when entering repetitive commands or correcting typing mistakes. These keys affect whatever command is currently stored in the *command line buffer*, a portion of RAM used to save and recall the most recently entered command. Only one command at a time is stored in this buffer, unless you are using a special utility like DOSKEY. (Notice that this buffer is not the same as the *active command line*, which displays command information on the screen as it is entered.) The following list describes these special function keys:

F1 or →
(right arrow key)

Enters the first character from the command line buffer on the active command line. DOS remembers its current position within the buffer: if you press F1 again, the next character will appear on the active command line. It is possible to enter the entire contents of the buffer, one character at a time, by repeatedly pressing this key.

F2, then *x*

Enters all the characters from the buffer starting at the current buffer position up to (but not including) the first occurrence of *x*, which is any single character you specify. This is useful for reentering commands in which a single character must be overwritten or added. If the specified character cannot be found in the buffer, this key has no effect.

F3

Enters all the remaining characters in the command buffer, starting from the current cursor position. This key is useful when repeating whole commands with little or no modification.

F4, then *x*

Skips over all the characters in the command line buffer up to the specified character *x*, then enters that character on the command line when you press F1 or →. If you press F3 after entering the character, the remaining portion of the command line buffer is displayed. If the specified character does not appear in the command buffer, this key has no effect.

F5	Replaces the command line buffer with the contents of the active command line. Is also useful for correcting typing errors at the beginning of the command line. For example, imagine you have entered the following incorrect command:

CCOPY A: B:

To correct the typo quickly, press F5, type an *x*, and press F3 to finish the command. The F5 function key also has a special meaning when DOS 6 first loads into memory. Refer to *Part Two* for details.

Insert	Switches to Insert mode, whereupon characters you type from the keyboard will be added to the command line buffer at the cursor position, rather than overwriting the character at that position. Press F1, →, or F3 to display the remaining portion of the command line buffer.
Delete	Deletes the character in the current buffer position. This key must be pressed for each character you intend to delete.
Esc	Cancels changes you have made to the command line buffer and restores its original contents. This key must be pressed before you press the Enter key.
Backspace or ← (left arrow key)	Moves cursor to the left one position on the active command line and erases the character at that position. If the erased character was changed from the character in the buffer, the original character in the buffer is restored. If you are already at the beginning of the command line, this key has no effect.

Some application software packages take over the command line buffer for their own purposes or erase it altogether. If the function keys fail to produce characters on the active command line, it is likely that an application has cleared the command line buffer.

Certain key combinations are called *control keys*, because their functions become active when you hold down the Ctrl key and type a character. Control keys perform a number of useful services:

Ctrl-C	Stops a DOS command in mid-processing and returns to the DOS prompt. Ctrl-Break has the same effect.
Ctrl-H	Functions the same as Backspace.
Ctrl-P	Causes the console output to be sent to the printer as well as the screen. The printer must be online or the system may cease functioning, at least until the printer is brought online. When the printer is online, pressing this control key a second time will turn the printer echo off.
Ctrl-S	Pauses the execution of the DOS command. Useful when large amounts of data flow beyond the boundaries of the screen. If your keyboard has a Pause key, this key will do the same thing. To resume processing, press any key (except Ctrl-C or a function key).
Shift-PrtSc	Sends the current contents of the screen to the printer.

FILE NAMES

Files are the heart of a DOS system. Related information such as a letter, book chapter, spreadsheet, database, or application program is stored under a unique *file name*. A file name is 1–8 characters long and may include a *file extension* at the end, which is a period followed by 3 more characters.

Legal characters in file names include all letters of the alphabet (upper- and lowercase are treated the same), numeric digits, and punctuation marks, except for the following:

    * ? = + | [ ] ; / < > , "

WILDCARD CHARACTERS

DOS supports two wildcard characters, ? (question mark) and * (asterisk), that allow you to specify whole groups of file names. The ? stands for any single character in the specified position within the file name or extension, and the * stands for any set of characters, starting at the specified position within the name or extension and continuing to the end of the file name or extension.

For example, the following syntax displays all files names on drive A that begin with any two characters followed by *001* and any extension:

    DIR A:??001.*

The following syntax displays the names of all files on the default drive:

    DIR *.*

REDIRECTING OUTPUT

Many DOS commands display messages of some sort. Normally these messages appear on your monitor screen. However, it is possible to direct the output of DOS commands to another device or to a disk file by means of a *redirection symbol* followed by a *target*.

The redirection symbol for output is the *closing brace* (}), or *greater-than sign* (>).

Standard target device names are as follows:

CON	The console, or screen display (the default)
PRN	The default printing device
LPT1	Parallel printer port #1
LPT2	Parallel printer port #2
COM1	Communications port #1
COM2	Communications port #2
COM3	Communications port #3
COM4	Communications port #4
AUX	An auxiliary output device
NUL	Null device (suppresses output from the command)

In addition to these standard device names, you may redirect output to a file name. If the file that you name does not exist, it is created. If it exists, it will be overwritten. If you want to add to an existing file instead of overwriting it, double the redirection symbol: >>

For example:

    DIR > PRN

lists a directory of the current drive and sends the output to the standard printing device.

    DIR > DIRFILE.TXT

sends the output to a file named DIRFILE.TXT.

    DIR >> DIRFILE.TXT

adds the output from the DIR command to the contents of the file DIRFILE.TXT.

REDIRECTING INPUT

Many DOS commands accept input of one sort or another. Normally, the user enters this input with the keyboard. If the keystrokes that make up this input are capable of being stored in a disk file, DOS can read the file and accept its contents just as if the keystrokes had been typed. This is useful in reducing the margin of error in repetitive tasks. Command input may also be accepted from any device that is capable of supplying data to DOS, such as COM1–COM4 or AUX.

The redirection symbol for input is the *opening brace* (⟨), or *less-than sign* (<).

For example, the MORE command will accept input from a file on disk. The MORE command displays characters on the screen, but if the number of lines is greater than the available screen display, the MORE command pauses and waits for the user to press a key before continuing the display. This prevents characters from scrolling off the screen before the operator has a chance to read them.

    MORE < LONGFILE.TXT

displays the contents of LONGFILE.TXT, pausing each time the screen fills.

For another example, consider the CHKDSK/F command, which checks the condition of a data disk. If problems are found, DOS prompts you to enter *Y* or *N* to confirm that you would like DOS to fix the problems it has found. If you intend always to answer Y, you can create a small text file on disk that contains only the letter Y, followed by Enter. You may call this tiny file Y.TXT. Then, the following command line (which you might place in a batch file) is valid:

    CHKDSK/F < Y.TXT

CHKDSK/F, instead of pausing and prompting you for a response, takes the response from the disk file instead.

PIPING

Many DOS commands produce output that can be reprocessed by other DOS commands. One way to do this is to redirect the output to a disk file, and then send the contents of the file as input to the next DOS command.

However, DOS allows a more convenient means of accomplishing this, by permitting you to combine multiple commands on a single command line. This technique is called *piping*, named after the "pipe" character used to combine DOS commands: | .

The piping technique works as follows: the output of one DOS command is sent to another DOS command, which in turn processes the output it receives and then either sends it to yet another DOS command or displays the final output. Here are some examples:

CHKDSK /V | MORE

sends the output from the CHKDSK /V command (oftentimes a long list of file names) to the MORE command, which pauses the display of the list each time the screen fills.

CHKDSK C: /V | FIND "COMMAND.COM"

sends the output from the CHKDSK C: /V command to the FIND command, which extracts and displays all occurrences of the file name COMMAND.COM. If you try this command yourself, be sure that you specify the file name entirely in uppercase characters.

DIR C: | SORT | MORE

sends the output of the DIR command to the SORT command, which sorts the file list in alphabetical order, then sends the output to the MORE command, which pauses the display each time the screen fills with file names.

BACKING UP YOUR DATA

This is the prime directive of all computer users; every experienced user knows well to abide by it. Nevertheless, even in this enlightened age, a few unfortunate users will wait until they lose important data before they discover the wisdom of making routine backups.

Computer storage systems hold vast amounts of data that can be wiped out by a technical glitch or careless command entry. If you have current backups of your data, this is usually no more than a temporary annoyance. If you do not have backups, however, it can be an ugly disaster.

Backing up is not difficult, and if you do it regularly, it need not be overly time-consuming. Once you have incorporated a regular system of backing up your data files, the process will fit seamlessly into your daily computing routine. The important thing is to make data backups part of your working habits. Refer to the MSBACKUP command in *Part Four* for details.

Here's an important tip regarding backups: make them before you experience a problem, not after. If you suddenly discover a problem with your data, there is usually no good purpose in overwriting your current backup disk with another backup; you might replace good data on your backup disk with bad data. If you want to make a copy of your data after you have discovered a problem, do so on a separate set of floppy disks.

You should always have at least one current backup of your data; two backups are preferable. They should be kept in a secure location away from your computer. This will give you the necessary sense of security to experiment with the DOS commands described in this book. Most DOS mistakes will not be destructive; commands with potential to lose data (such as ERASE or COPY) are duly noted in the text.

Part Two

Installing and Configuring DOS 6

Configuring your system for DOS 6 requires that you first install the operating system software on your hard disk (or startup diskette if your system does not have a hard disk). After installing DOS 6, you probably will want to configure the operating system to make the most of the unique components of your system; for example, the amount and type of random-access memory (RAM) you are using, how your data storage disks are organized, requirements made on the operating system by internal and external peripheral devices like monitors, special keyboards, printers, modems, and the like.

Hardware systems vary widely and can contain a vast number of combinations of external and internal devices. The advantage to the architecture of DOS-compatible computers is such that much leeway is left to you to make the most of the operating system's ability to manage all the various possible combinations of hardware components.

It is extremely important that you have a sound understanding of the current hardware and software components of your system before attempting to install DOS 6. At a minimum, you should make a complete backup of all data on your hard disk, or any data disk you will be using to store DOS 6 files. Read that portion of the DOS 6 documentation that deals with installation issues (*Getting Started*) and keep those instructions handy during the process.

In addition, you should take the following pre-installation steps if required:

- Be certain you have up to 4 Mb of free disk space on your hard disk, if you are installing DOS 6 there. You may not need this much room, depending on whether you are installing DOS 6 for the DOS prompt, Windows, or both, but if the space is there or you can make it available, you will assure yourself of a smoother installation process.

- Prepare a blank diskette, labeled *Uninstall Disk*. You will use this disk during installation, and you will need it later if you decide you want to restore your previous version of DOS. If you are using low-density disks (360K or less), you may need two Uninstall disks.

- If you are installing on floppy disks, prepare additional disks labeled as follows:

  - Startup & Support
  - Help, QuickBASIC, Editor, & Utility
  - Supplemental

- Disable any current virus-protection, deletion-protection, password-protection, network pop-up message services, or disk- caching programs that are currently running on your system. These applications may conflict with the setup process. Even though they may not, it is better to play it safe. Disabling these programs may require that you make changes to your CONFIG.SYS and AUTOEXEC.BAT files. If you are uncertain how to do this, do not attempt to install the software. Instead, refer the job to a qualified associate.

This chapter describes the fundamentals of installing and configuring DOS 6.

INSTALLING DOS 6

DOS 6 includes an automated installation routine that is suitable for most standard systems. Unless your system is non-standard in some way, you should be able to use this automated routine to transfer DOS 6 to your system. To access the automated routine, put the DOS 6 setup disk in your system's floppy disk drive, log onto that drive and enter the following command:

SETUP

The automated installation routine will analyze your system and display a series of information screens and menus that inform you of the steps you need to take to complete the installation process. Read each screen and answer each prompt carefully. If you are unsure how to respond to a prompt, refer to your documentation or ask a qualified associate.

Be especially careful if any of the following apply to you:

- You are currently running OS/2 on your system. You may be required to remove OS/2 first. Refer to your documentation for details.

- You are currently running Windows on your system. The installation procedure looks for Windows and makes certain changes to its configuration file, if required by your system. You will also be offered the option of installing DOS 6 backup, undelete, and anti-virus utilities for Windows or the DOS prompt, or both.

- You are currently using a disk-compression system on your hard disk. If so, you can install DOS 6 but you will not be able to use the Uninstall disks. If you decide later to remove DOS 6, you will be required to restore your data from the backup you made before you started.

- Your hard disk is not partitioned in a standard format. In such a case, you must refer to your documentation for special instructions and might possibly have to contact Microsoft Product Support. Some examples of manufacturers and operating systems that employ non-standard hard disk partitions are:

  - Bernoulli
  - Everex
  - Novell
  - Ontrack Disk Manager
  - Priam
  - SyQuest (removable hard disk)
  - UNIX
  - Vfeature Deluxe
  - XENIX

  If you find that you need to repartition your hard disk, refer to your documentation or have the job done by a qualified systems person. The DOS 6 installation documentation includes detailed information on repartitioning your hard disk, which is beyond the scope of this book. By all means, make a backup of your data and assure yourself of its reliability before proceeding.

UNINSTALLING DOS 6

If after completing the installation process, you decide you want to restore your previous version of DOS, insert your Uninstall disk in your floppy-disk drive, reboot your computer by pressing **Ctrl-Alt-Del**, and follow the instructions that appear on your screen.

The automated installation routine saves the files from your previous version of DOS on a special disk directory named OLD_DOS.1. The uninstall routine requires that the files on this directory exist in order to restore your previous version of DOS.

You cannot use the Uninstall disk, or restore your previous version of DOS, after you have done any of the following:

- Deleted files on the OLD_DOS.1 directory

- Deleted or moved DOS's system files (IO.SYS and MSDOS.SYS)

- Installed a disk-compression program (including the DoubleSpace utility supplied with DOS 6)

- Repartitioned or reformatted your hard disk

CONFIGURING WITH MEMMAKER

The simplest way to optimize and configure DOS 6 for your system is to use the Memmaker utility supplied with the operating system. This application analyzes your system and rewrites the CONFIG.SYS file to make optimal use of your system's resources. Like the installation routine, it presents you with several screens of information and prompts you to make choices. On most standard systems, you should accept the default responses. Memmaker includes recovery procedures if you do not like the results or if any of your applications work incorrectly after you run it. To run Memmaker, log onto your DOS 6 directory and enter the following at the DOS prompt:

MEMMAKER

Carefully follow the instructions on your screen. These instructions vary from system to system; for example, Memmaker will substitute EMM386.EXE for third-party expanded-memory managers on you system. Memmaker stores the original versions of CONFIG.SYS and AUTOEXEC.BAT in your DOS directory with the names CONFIG.UMB and AUTOEXEC.UMB. The Memmaker command will also alter the file SYSTEM.INI if Windows is present on your system. A backup of the original SYSTEM.INI is saved as SYSTEM.UMB. If you must recover your old configuration manually, copy these files to your root directory as CONFIG.SYS and AUTOEXEC.BAT, respectively. For more details, refer to the MEMMAKER command in *Part Four*.

CONFIGURING WITH CONFIG.SYS

CONFIG.SYS is an ASCII file that contains instructions to DOS for making best use of your system's resources. Because it is an ASCII file, you can edit it manually using a text editor such as the one brought up by the EDIT command. You must be familiar with the command syntax employed by CONFIG.SYS and the purposes of the various software utilities that can be installed by means of this file. For a synopsis of CONFIG.SYS syntax, refer to *Appendix A*. For a description of various files (called *driver files*) supplied with DOS 6 and used by CONFIG.SYS, refer to *Appendix C*. For advanced information on modifying CONFIG.SYS to allow you to choose between different configurations at startup time, refer to the *Multiple Configurations* section just ahead in this chapter.

CONFIGURING WITH AUTOEXEC.BAT

The AUTOEXEC.BAT file is an ASCII file that contains a series of DOS line commands, which will be invoked in sequence automatically at startup time. Although it can contain any command that can be validly invoked at the DOS prompt, its usual purpose is to invoke additional configuration commands and startup programs that you would otherwise invoke yourself each time you started your computer. Because AUTOEXEC.BAT is an ASCII file, you can edit it manually using a text editor such as the one brought up by the EDIT command. You must be familiar with DOS line commands and batch files in general to edit this file effectively. For more information about batch file syntax, refer to *Appendix B* of this book.

MULTIPLE CONFIGURATIONS

DOS 6 includes a special feature that allows you to write CON-FIG.SYS so that you can choose among multiple configurations at startup time. For example, consider RAM disks. A RAM disk is a special area of random-access memory that appears to the operating system to be another disk drive. Its advantage is that it is often faster than physical disk drives, or more convenient for storing temporary files. (Bear in mind that data stored on a RAM disk must be saved to a physical drive before the computer is shut down, or it will be lost).

RAM disks are initialized using CONFIG.SYS. There may be times when you want a RAM disk and other times when you would prefer not to use up valuable RAM that might be better used by one or more of your applications. Prior to DOS 6, you would be required to edit the CONFIG.SYS file and restart your computer to add or delete a RAM disk. In DOS 6, you can restart the computer and choose whether or not to include the RAM disk (or any other configuration option you like) from a menu on the screen.

Before attempting to rewrite your CONFIG.SYS file to support multiple configurations, you must be familiar with standard CONFIG.SYS syntax and how to use driver files. *Appendix A* summarizes fundamental CONFIG.SYS syntax, and DOS 6 driver files are described in *Appendix C*. Multiple-configuration CONFIG.SYS files utilize this fundamental syntax plus some additional elements: menu blocks, configuration blocks, include directives, and a common block.

The general structure of a multiple-configuration CONFIG.SYS file is as follows:

1. A sequence of required commands, if any, that must be invoked first, regardless of which option is to be selected.

2. An initial menu block, always named [menu], containing up to nine configuration choices for the user.

3. Any number of configuration blocks that contain commands referenced in optional configuration blocks.

4. The series of optional configuration blocks, containing the commands required for each optional selection from the menu.

5. A final common configuration block, always named [common], which is always the last configuration block in the file. This block contains configuration commands that are always invoked, regardless of which option is chosen, but must follow the optional configuration blocks in the file.

In addition, a multiple-configuration CONFIG.SYS file may contain *submenus*. A submenu is another configuration block with a unique block name of your choosing that contains additional menu commands. It is referenced like any other configuration block, but functions like an additional, nested menu. Use submenus if you require more than nine optional configurations or if you feel that submenus organize your possible choices more logically than a single menu.

Listing 2.1 is a simple multiple-configuration CONFIG.SYS file that demonstrates a typical structure. The elements in this file are explained more fully in the following sections.

```
rem **  These commands are used by all options:
DEVICE=C:\SW\DOS\HIMEM.SYS
DOS=HIGH
rem **  This is the configuration menu:
[menu]
MENUCOLOR=15,1
MENUITEM=ramdisk1,RAM disk (1024Kb)
MENUITEM=ramdisk2,RAM disk (2048Kb)
MENUITEM=noramdisk,No RAM disk
MENUDEFAULT=noramdisk,15
rem ** This is the configuration block that initializes
rem ** expanded memory to validate the DEVICEHIGH command:
[expanded]
DEVICE=EMM386.EXE RAM HIGHSCAN
rem ** These are the optional RAM disk configuration commands:
[ramdisk1]
INCLUDE=expanded
DEVICEHIGH=C:\DOS\RAMDRIVE.SYS 1024 512 512 /E
[ramdisk2]
INCLUDE=expanded
DEVICEHIGH=C:\DOS\RAMDRIVE.SYS 2048 512 512 /E
rem **  The noramdisk block is empty, because no RAM disk is
rem **  initialized, and thus no command is needed:

[noramdisk]
rem **  "Common" block, currently empty:
[common]
```

Listing 2.1: A multiple-configuration CONFIG.SYS file

MENU BLOCKS

A *menu block* is a series of commands in CONFIG.SYS that describe a simple menu of options to be displayed on the screen. The series of commands is preceded by a *menu block name,* an identifying word enclosed in square brackets. For example, a multiple-configuration CONFIG.SYS file requires at least one menu block, identified by the menu block name *menu*, on its own line, as follows:

    [menu]

When DOS encounters this line in CONFIG.SYS syntax, it treats it as an instruction to display a startup menu on the screen. This menu block name is followed by a series of special commands that indicate what is to be included in the menu. The commands following the menu block name begin with the command keyword *MENUITEM*, as in the following example:

    [menu]
    MENUITEM=ramdisk1,RAM disk (1024Kb)
    MENUITEM=ramdisk2,RAM disk (2048Kb)
    MENUITEM=noramdisk,No RAM disk

Notice that the MENUITEM keyword is followed by an equals sign (=) and two additional parameters, separated by a comma. The first parameter is a *configuration block name*, which will be explained shortly. The second parameter is optional text to be displayed on the screen, a prompt that tells the user the type of configuration that will be accessed if this menu item is selected. This menu block will then cause DOS to display the following menu when you start your computer:

    MS-DOS 6 Startup Menu
    =======================
       1. RAM Disk (1024Kb)
       2. RAM Disk (2048Kb)
       3. No RAM Disk
    Enter a choice:

You can select one of the options by entering the menu number, or by moving a highlighted bar to the desired option, and pressing Enter.

ENHANCING THE MENU BLOCK

You can use two CONFIG.SYS commands to enhance your menu block. The first, MENUCOLOR, allows you to instruct DOS to display the menu using specified text and background colors (if your system is equipped with a color monitor). More details on this command and the available color codes may be found in *Appendix A*.

The second command, MENUDEFAULT, instructs DOS to make one of the menu items the default selection and select it automatically after a specified number of seconds (in the range from 0 to 90). Again, refer to *Appendix A* for more detailed information on this command.

Adding these commands to our example menu yields the following revised menu block:

```
[menu]
MENUCOLOR=15,1
MENUITEM=ramdisk1,RAM disk (1024Kb)
MENUITEM=ramdisk2,RAM disk (2048Kb)
MENUITEM=noramdisk,No RAM disk
MENUDEFAULT=noramdisk,15
```

making the menu white on a blue background and specifying *noramdisk* as the default configuration block, to be automatically selected if the user does not make a selection after approximately 15 seconds.

CONFIGURATION BLOCKS

A *configuration block* is a series of CONFIG.SYS commands that are preceded by a *configuration block name*. Like a menu block name, a configuration block name is a keyword enclosed in brackets. The keyword may be any character series you like, but for clarity you should make it brief and descriptive. In the previous menu block, three configuration block names were referenced: *ramdisk1* (for the first RAM disk); *ramdisk2* (for the second RAM disk); and *noramdisk* (for no ram disk). The CONFIG.SYS file must contain these configuration block names followed by their associated CONFIG.SYS commands.

Bear in mind that all CONFIG.SYS commands following a configuration block name are considered part of the referenced configuration block, until another configuration block name is encountered in the file. For example, the following examples, although cumbersome, would be valid configuration blocks using the example names, initializing extended memory, loading DOS in the high memory area, and optionally initializing the RAM disks:

```
[ramdisk1]
DEVICE=C:\DOS\HIMEM.SYS
DEVICE=C:\DOS\EMM386.EXE RAM HIGHSCAN
DEVICEHIGH=C:\DOS\RAMDRIVE.SYS 1024 512 512 /E
[ramdisk2]
DEVICE=C:\DOS\HIMEM.SYS
DEVICE=C:\DOS\EMM386.EXE RAM HIGHSCAN
DEVICEHIGH=C:\DOS\RAMDRIVE.SYS 2048 512 512 /E
[noramdisk]
DEVICE=C:\DOS\HIMEM.SYS
```

INCLUDE DIRECTIVES

Notice that, because the RAM disk drivers in the above example are loaded into upper memory using the DEVICEHIGH command, it was necessary to initialize HIMEM.SYS and EMM386.EXE before the RAM disk can be initialized. In the above example, however, this two-line sequence was repeated in each configuration block, which is cumbersome. There is a better way.

To make the CONFIG.SYS file more efficient and avoid copying duplicate syntax lines throughout, DOS 6 allows you to gather these common commands into their own configuration blocks and reference these blocks instead of copying the lines. Using the INCLUDE

command, you could rewrite the previous example as shown in the
following example:

```
[expanded]
DEVICE=EMM386.EXE RAM HIGHSCAN
[ramdisk1]
INCLUDE=expanded
DEVICEHIGH=C:\DOS\RAMDRIVE.SYS 1024 512 512 /E
[ramdisk2]
INCLUDE=expanded
DEVICEHIGH=C:\DOS\RAMDRIVE.SYS 2048 512 512 /E
[noramdisk]
```

In Listing 2.1, the DEVICE=HIMEM.SYS line was moved to the
beginning of the file, before any menu or configuration blocks.
After the menu block, a new configuration block was added,
named [expanded], which contained the line to initialize expanded
memory. This line was then referenced in the configuration blocks
that used the DEVICEHIGH command. Notice that, if *noramdisk* is
the selected configuration block, the expanded memory driver is
not initialized, conserving a small amount of conventional memory
for applications.

Notice that include directives are not necessary for CONFIG.SYS
commands that are common to all options. Simply place these commands first in the file, without a configuration block name.

THE COMMON BLOCK

If common commands must follow the optional commands in the
CONFIG.SYS file, you can place them in their own configuration block
in the end of the file, named [common]. DOS recognizes this block as a
group of CONFIG.SYS commands that are invoked always, but must
be invoked *after* one of the optional blocks is invoked.

Even if your CONFIG.SYS file has no common commands at the
end, it is a good practice to end the CONFIG.SYS file with the [com-
mon] block name, in case any subsequent application you install attempts to add its own configuration lines to the CONFIG.SYS file.

CONFIGURATION OPTIONS IN AUTOEXEC.BAT

It is entirely possible that options selected from a CONFIG.SYS menu will affect commands invoked in the AUTOEXEC.BAT file. DOS 6 provides a simple mechanism for allowing AUTOEXEC.BAT (or any other batch file, for that matter) to make choices between various commands, based on the user's configuration selection. When a multiple-configuration CONFIG.SYS file is used, DOS stores the block name of the selected configuration block in a special environment variable named CONFIG. For example, if the user selected [noramdisk] in the above example, CONFIG would be automatically set to equal *noramdisk*. Based on the value of the CONFIG variable, AUTOEXEC.BAT can include lines to use or not use the RAM disk:

```
IF %CONFIG%==noramdisk SET TEMP=C:\TEMP
rem ** The RAM disk, if initialized, will be drive D:
IF NOT %CONFIG%==noramdisk SET TEMP=D:\
```

If the RAM disk does not exist, the value of the TEMP environment variable is set to equal the \TEMP directory on drive C. If the RAM disk exists, the value of TEMP is set to equal the root directory of the RAM disk, drive D.

Any batch file command, including commands to go to different labels in the file, can be used based on the value of the CONFIG variable. Refer to *Appendix B* for more information on batch-file syntax.

DEBUGGING MULTIPLE-CONFIGURATION FILES

If you experience problems when writing a multiple-configuration CONFIG.SYS file, your system may hang, or become impossible to boot. DOS 6 includes a mechanism for getting past problem lines in CONFIG.SYS, or ignoring it altogether.

When DOS 6 first loads at startup time, it displays the message "Starting MS-DOS..." When you see this message, you may do one of the following immediately:

1. Press the **F5** function key. This causes DOS 6 to bypass the CONFIG.SYS and AUTOEXEC.BAT files entirely, loading a bland, default version of DOS.

2. Press the **F8** function key. This causes DOS 6 to invoke the lines in CONFIG.SYS one-by-one, asking you to confirm each one by pressing Y to invoke the line or N to bypass it. Then, DOS offers you the choice whether to process AUTOEXEC.BAT or ignore it, again by pressing Y to process or N to ignore.

Either option allows you to bypass troublesome lines in CON-FIG.SYS and AUTOEXEC.BAT, start your computer, make the necessary modifications to the file, and restart. These function keys are also available to you when the startup menu appears on the screen.

Part Three

The DOS Shell

DOS's abstract line commands and its minimal prompting use computer resources efficiently; however, this approach often forces the user to memorize arcane commands and parameters. Many users are comfortable with DOS's line command and C prompt; other users who would rather work in a more concrete and intuitive environment will appreciate an important feature that first appeared in DOS 4.0: a graphic user interface called the *DOS shell*.

The DOS shell allows you to perform a wide variety of everyday file management tasks in a more intuitive way. For example, you can

- Maintain an ongoing display of your hard disk's directory structure plus lists of files within each directory.

- Launch an application program by pointing to a data file you have associated with it.

- Move, copy, and delete data files in a graphic, menu-driven context.

In addition to these more traditional tasks, the DOS shell allows you to do something that is impossible at the DOS prompt: hold more than one open application program in RAM at a time and switch between them.

This chapter briefly outlines the shell's features.

THE SHELL DISPLAY

Load the DOS shell by typing **DOSSHELL** at the DOS prompt. If you plan to use the DOS shell frequently, you may want to include the command as the last line in your AUTOEXEC.BAT file. After you invoke the command you will see a display similar to the one pictured in Figure 3.1.

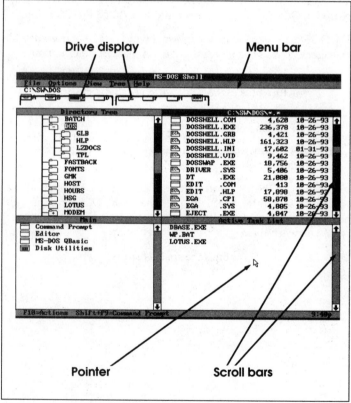

Figure 3.1: The DOS shell

The following sections describe the main features of the shell and how to use them.

THE POINTER

The *pointer* is a small icon that moves about the screen. You control its movements by means of a peripheral device such as a mouse, trackball (a ball that records movement as you rotate it in place), or the arrow keys on the keyboard. Although all the features of the DOS shell are accessible by means of the keyboard, this is the least efficient means of using the shell, and a mouse or trackball is recommended. For the sake of simplicity, this text refers to any tracking device as a mouse.

A mouse includes at least one button, called the *pick button*. The DOS shell makes use of only this one button. If your mouse has more than one button, you may have to experiment with your device to determine which is the pick button.

You can use either the mouse or the keyboard to move the pointer between the various windows, select menu commands or file names, start applications, or change drives and directories. If you are not using a mouse, you may use the **Tab** key to highlight different windows in sequential order and the keyboard's arrow keys to move the pointer between highlighted items in a selected window. You may select an item by pressing the **spacebar** or **Enter**.

HIGHLIGHTING AND SELECTING ITEMS

Several terms in this chapter are used frequently to refer to highlighting and selecting items in the DOS shell:

An item is *highlighted* when it appears in a different or reverse color. To highlight items, touch them with the pointer and press the pick button. If you are using the keyboard, move the highlight bar using the keyboard's arrow keys.

To *pick*, or *select*, an item, touch it with the pointer and press the pick button once. To accomplish the same thing using the keyboard, move the highlight bar with the arrow keys and press the spacebar.

To *double-click* on an item, move the pointer to it and quickly press the pick button twice. To accomplish the same thing using the keyboard, move the highlight bar with the arrow keys and press Enter.

Refer to the section later in *Part Three* entitled *The File Display* for other techniques to use when picking file names.

In certain circumstances, you may need to move the mouse while holding the pick button down. For example, you use this technique to start applications with default files. To do this, first pick the default file. Then, while holding the pick button down, move the pointer to the application file name (a file with the extension .COM, .EXE, or .BAT). If the application can be successfully launched with the selected data file, the pointer icon will be replaced by the data file's icon. If the application cannot be successfully launched, the pointer arrow is replaced by a small circle with a diagonal line through the center.

THE MENU BAR

The *menu bar* is the first active line on the DOS shell screen. It contains *keywords* that activate pull-down menus of various operating system commands. These menus and their associated commands are described in more detail later in *Part Three*.

To activate a menu, highlight the associated keyword, then press the pick button. If you are using the keyboard, activate the pull-down menus by holding down the **Alt** key and pressing the first letter of the keyword. For example, to activate the File pull-down menu, press Alt-F. Alternatively, you can access the menu bar by pressing the **F10** function key and moving between the keywords with the arrow keys.

DIALOG BOXES

When you invoke certain commands in the DOS Shell, a *dialog box* will appear. An example of a dialog box appears in Figure 3.2. Dialog boxes contain prompts for different parameters associated with the shell command. For example, a dialog box may contain one or more *labels*, each followed by a *data field*. You can move between data fields by selecting them or using the keyboard arrow keys or **Tab** key. Type the appropriate command parameters in the data fields as indicated by the label.

To edit existing text in a data field, press the **Backspace** key or simply begin typing it in (which will blank the data field if the text is highlighted). Alternatively, you can edit the displayed directory path by pressing the left arrow key, which moves the cursor back through the field. Insert new characters by typing them, or delete characters at the cursor position by pressing the **Delete** key. Press the **Insert** key to toggle between inserting characters and overwriting them.

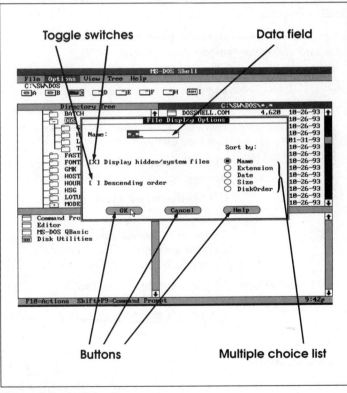

Figure 3.2: A dialog box

Certain dialog box options are represented by a *toggle switch*, in cases where a command option may be either active or inactive. A toggle switch appears in a dialog box as a label preceded by a pair of brackets ([]). When you select the brackets, an *X* either appears or disappears, indicating that the option is either active or inactive. DOS saves the current state of all toggle switches and presents them as the default the next time the dialog box appears.

If you are to choose one option from among several possibilities, the dialog box will display a *multiple choice list.* This list appears as a column of labels with a small circle to the left of each. Choose one option by selecting the circle. The selected circle fills, indicating that the option is chosen. You may pick only one option from the list; picking one automatically clears whatever is currently chosen.

Most dialog boxes contain other command switches called *buttons.* Standard dialog box buttons are as follows:

OK	Accepts the chosen dialog box parameters and either executes the command or causes another dialog box to appear
BACK	Backs up, one at a time, through a series of nested dialog boxes
CLOSE	Closes the current window and returns to the shell without taking any other action
CANCEL	Cancels the command and returns to the shell
HELP	Temporarily suspends the command and displays a window of information regarding the current command
ADVANCED...	Displays a second dialog box of additional parameters that are used in special circumstances

SCROLL BARS

When a dialog box or window contains text or a data list that is too large to fit, a *scroll bar* will appear to the right of the display. Scroll bars are illustrated in Figure 3.1, just to the right of the Directory

Tree window and the File Display window. A scroll bar is a vertical bar with an arrow at the top and bottom and a small rectangle inside. You can use the scroll bar to scroll the display within a window or dialog box by one of several means:

- *Pick an Arrow with the Pointer.* Selecting the top arrow will scroll the display up, the bottom arrow will scroll it down. If you select the arrow and hold the pick button down, the display will scroll continuously.

- *Move the Small Rectangle in the Scroll Bar.* Select the rectangle with the pointer and hold the pick button down. As you move the pointer up and down, you move the rectangle within the scroll bar, and the display within the dialog box will scroll up and down, following the movements of the rectangle.

- *Press the PgUp or PgDn Key* to scroll the display one screenful at a time.

- *Press the Up or Down Arrow Key* to scroll the display one line at a time.

THE DRIVE DISPLAY

The *drive display* appears just under the menu bar. It shows which drives are available in the system. In the DOS shell's graphics display, the drives are represented by a drive letter followed by an *icon,* a small picture, that indicates the type of drive associated with each letter. If the drive is a floppy-disk drive, the drive icon includes a drive bay door. If the drive is a hard-disk drive, the icon does not include the door catch. If the drive is a RAM disk, the icon appears as a small memory chip. Refer to Figure 3.1 for an illustration of each of these icons.

To make a drive active, move the pointer to the desired drive letter and press the pick button. If you are using the keyboard, move the pointer using the keyboard's arrow keys and press the **spacebar**.

THE DIRECTORY TREE

The *directory tree window* displays the directory structure of the currently active drive. To log onto a particular directory, move the pointer to it and select it.

Each directory is accompanied by an icon that looks like a little file folder or square brackets, depending on your display. If there are subdirectories nested below a given directory, the icon will contain a small plus symbol (+). You may display these nested subdirectories by picking the icon. If you are using the keyboard, highlight the directory and press the **plus** key.

If the nested subdirectories are currently displayed, the icon of the parent directory contains a minus sign (–). To close the directory, pick the icon containing the minus sign. If you are using the keyboard, highlight the directory and press the **minus** key.

THE FILE DISPLAY

The files in the currently active directory are displayed in the *file display window*. A small icon appears to the left of each file name. If the file is an executable program, the icon appears as a small rectangle with a horizontal line near the top. If the file is a data file, the icon appears as a sheet of paper with the top right corner folded over.

You may launch an application program by double-clicking on it or, if using the keyboard, by highlighting it and pressing **Enter**.

Data files may be selected singly or in groups for any file-management operation such as copying, moving, deleting, and so forth. Use the procedure outlined later in *Part Three* in the section *Highlighting and Selecting Items* to select a single file. If you are using the keyboard, moving the pointer to a file name automatically selects it.

If you want to select a group of files, select the first file, then move the pointer to the next desired file. Hold down the **Ctrl** key on the keyboard and select the next file. Continue to select files while holding down the Ctrl key, until all desired files are highlighted. This method requires a mouse.

If you are using the keyboard only, you may select a series of files by holding down both the **Shift** key and the **spacebar** and moving the pointer with the up or down arrow key.

If you want to include all the files in a directory, choose Select All from the File pull-down menu or, if using the keyboard, hold down the **Ctrl** key and press the **forward-slash** (/) key.

If you want to deselect the chosen files, select another file. If you want to deselect files without selecting another file, choose Deselect all from the File menu or, if using the keyboard, hold down the **Ctrl** key and press the **backslash** (\) key.

When you have selected the desired data files, pick the appropriate DOS file-management command from one of the pull-down menus.

THE PROGRAM WINDOW

The *program window* lists available application software commands, called *program items*, or the names of other groups of program items, called *program groups*, nesting in their own window below the current one. In the shell's graphics display, program items appear with a small rectangular icon to the left of the name. Program groups have a similar icon that contains a small window symbol.

The standard version of the DOS shell includes three program items: the command prompt; the DOS text editor; and the Microsoft QuickBASIC programming environment; plus one program group, which is called Disk Utilities. This group contains a short list of program items that handle fundamental file management tasks: backing up files, restoring files from backup, formatting and copying disks, and undeleting files.

You may configure any current program window to include other program groups or items. To add a new program group or item, highlight the program window and pick the New command from the File menu. When you select this command, a dialog box appears offering you a choice between a program group or program item. If you pick a program group, it will be nested below the current program window. If you pick a program item, it will appear in the currently active program window.

After you select one or the other and select the **OK** button, additional dialog boxes will appear, depending on your selection.

If you choose to create a program group, a dialog box appears with the following prompts:

Title　　Enter a title for the program group as you would like it to appear in the program window. The title can be no more than 74 characters.

Help Text　　Enter the heading in the DOSSHELL.HLP file that contains help information for this program group if the heading appears in the file or you have modified the file to include it.

Password　　Enter a password to restrict access to this program group. If you enter a password here, you must re-enter it to open the program window or change any of its properties. Passwords are case-sensitive and must be entered exactly as specified in this data field.

If you choose to create a program item, a dialog box appears with the following prompts:

Program Title　　Enter a description of the program as you would like it to appear in the program window. This can be as simple as the program name itself, or a more detailed description up to a limit of 23 characters.

Commands　　Enter the DOS line command that will be invoked when this item is picked.

Startup Directory　　Enter the name of a directory that will be currently logged at the start of the application.

**Application
Shortcut Key**

Press a special key combination that can be used by the Task Swapper to switch directly to this application when multiple applications are active. This key combination is the equivalent of picking the program from the Active Task List window. Shortcut keys can be any keyboard key pressed while holding down either the **Shift** key, **Ctrl** key, or **Alt** key, provided that they do not conflict with any of the current application's command keys. For example, to switch to the program by pressing Shift-F1, move the cursor to this data box, hold down the **Shift** key and press the **F1** function key. The phrase *SHIFT-F1* will appear in the data box.

Pause After Exit

Activate this toggle switch if you would like DOS to display a "Press any key to continue" prompt upon leaving the application, but before returning to the shell. Deactivate this toggle switch if you would like to return to the shell immediately.

Password

Enter a password to restrict all access to this application. If you enter a password here, you must re-enter it to launch the application or change any of the program properties at a later time. Passwords are case-sensitive and must be entered exactly as specified in this data field.

If you select the **Advanced** button, a dialog box appears with the following prompts:

Help Text

Enter the heading in the DOSSHELL.HLP file that contains help information for this program group if the heading appears in the file or you have modified the file to include it.

Conventional Requirement

Enter the minimum amount of memory required by this application. If this field is left blank, all available memory will be used. Data in this field insures that sufficient memory is available before invoking the application. This information may be necessary if you intend to open several applications at once.

XMS Memory

Enter the minimum amount and upper limit of extended memory to be allocated for this application. These fields serve the same purpose as the previous field for applications that require a specific amount of extended memory to run.

Video Mode

You may pick either the Graphics or Text mode switches for programs that require a special video mode not used by the DOS shell. For example, select Graphics if your program requires graphics mode and you are running the shell in text mode.

Reserve Shortcut Keys

Select these toggle switches to indicate which key combinations may not be used by the shell to switch between this and other applications. If an X appears in the toggle box, the key combination is not available to the shell while this program is active. You should disable these if your application requires these special key combinations. If none are selected, you may use any of them to return to the shell while the program remains active. Be certain that the Task Swapper is enabled before attempting to switch between applications.

Prevent **Program** **Switch**	Select this toggle switch to disable program switching for this application. You should disable switching if attempting to keep this application open will cause conflicts with other applications.

After creating program items and groups, you may launch them by highlighting their names and picking the Open command from the File menu, double-clicking with the pointing device, or simply pressing Enter. If a program group is highlighted, opening it will activate it and display its contents in the program window area. If a program item is highlighted, opening it will invoke its associated command.

To reconfigure a program item or group, highlight it and select the Properties command from the File menu. If the program item or group is password protected, you must enter the password to modify the configuration. A dialog box appears showing the current settings for the program item or group. This dialog box is like the one displayed when you first created the program item or group. After making the appropriate changes to the settings, select the **OK** button or press **Enter**.

THE ACTIVE TASK LIST WINDOW

The *active task list window* is displayed if you have enabled the *Task Swapper,* a DOS shell feature that allows you to have several applications open at the same time. Each open application is listed in this window, and you may move from application to application by picking the application file name from the window. For more details regarding multiple open applications, refer to the *Task Swapping* section next.

TASK SWAPPING

When task swapping is enabled, you launch an application from within the shell, then suspend that application by pressing **Ctrl-Esc**, which returns you to the DOS shell. After returning to the DOS shell, you may launch another application, and repeat the process with as many applications as you have memory in your system to accommodate. Each application that remains suspended in memory is added to the list of applications in the Active Task List window.

To add an application to the Active Task List without launching it, highlight the application and press **Shift-Enter**. To remove an application from the list, exit it as you normally would using the application's own exit commands, instead suspending it by means of Ctrl-Esc.

You can move quickly from one application to the next on the list without returning to the shell. Several different key combinations will allow you to switch from the Shell to any application in the Active Task List, or switch between applications. The following list outlines these key combinations.

Key Combination	Function
Ctrl-Esc	Switches to the shell from an application
Alt-Esc	Switches to the next application on the Active Task List
Alt-Shift-Esc	Switches to the previous application on the Active Task List
Alt-Tab	Alternates between two applications

In addition, you may define a special shortcut key to bring up any application on the Active Task List. Refer to the *Program Window* section in *Part Three* for details on defining shortcut keys.

You cannot disable the Task Swapper or exit the shell while tasks are still active. Close all active applications first by entering them and ending the processing, using each application's normal exit routine. If you are at the DOS prompt or an exiting application has returned you to the DOS prompt, enter the EXIT command to return to the shell.

HELP WITH SHELL COMMANDS

The DOS shell provides context-sensitive help. You can access this help at any time while in the shell by pressing **F1**. If you press F1 while a menu command is highlighted, you will receive detailed information on that command.

You can access Help for various topics using the pull-down menu options discussed in this section. To reveal the Help menu, pick the Help keyword from the menu bar. Unlike other menus, the Help menu is fully available no matter which window in the shell is active.

When you access the Help feature, a *help dialog box* appears on the screen. You can scroll through the information in this dialog box using the scroll bar, or you can double-click on any related topic to reveal another dialog box of information. Related topics are easily identifiable, as they are displayed in a highlighted or otherwise contrasting color. You can continue to display as many help windows as you need in order to receive the information you are looking for.

The Help command is extremely flexible, and allows you to navigate throughout the various topics in a free-form way. Each help dialog box has a set of buttons that allow you to jump to commonly used areas:

CLOSE	Returns to the shell
BACK	Backs up through the previously displayed help dialog boxes, one at a time
KEYS	Displays topics related to the use of the keyboard
INDEX	Redisplays the Help Index
HELP	Displays information on using the Help feature

The following general categories are available from the Help menu:

ABOUT SHELL   Displays the DOS shell version number and copyright notice.

COMMANDS   Displays the shell's menu commands, listed in the same order that they appear on the screen and arranged by menu bar keyword. To get help with a command, scroll through the list and double- click on the command of your choice.

INDEX   Displays the Help Index, which covers general information about the DOS shell. The Help Index is similar in structure to the Help pull-down menu and allows you to access general categories of Shell features: Keyboard; Commands; Procedures; Shell Basics (such as manipulating windows and file lists, picking items, working with dialog boxes, and so forth); and using the Help feature itself.

KEYBOARD   Displays a selection of topics related to using the keyboard in the shell.

PROCEDURES   Displays topics related to file and program management, as well as configuration, customization, and more basic shell techniques.

SHELL BASICS   Displays a selection of topics on the fundamental shell techniques: displaying and picking file names; using dialog boxes; using menus, and so forth.

USING HELP   Displays information and related topics on how to access the help feature.

For example, to get help with managing multiple applications, select Help from the menu bar, followed by Index, and scroll through the dialog box until you reach the Commands Help section. Double-click on Options Menu, and you will find Enable Task Swapper Command. Double-click on this entry to see a brief description of the Task Swapper command, followed by other topics that present the information in more detail.

A simpler alternative to using the Help Index would be to activate the Options pull-down menu, move to the Enable Task Swapper command using the keyboard arrow keys, and, when the command is highlighted, press **F1**.

FILE MENU COMMANDS

This section lists the commands that appear when you pick the File keyword in the menu bar. These commands help manage files on disk and control the behavior of files within the DOS shell. For more details on individual commands, highlight the command in the menu and press the **F1** function key. Some commands are available only when certain shell windows are active. Some commands behave differently depending on which window is active. These differences are noted in the description of each command.

ASSOCIATE   Binds a file name to an application name
                           so the application is launched when the
                           file name is picked. This command is
                           available only when the File Display
                           window is active.

CHANGE   Permits you to change the attributes of
ATTRIBUTES   files. If you are unfamiliar with the
                           concept of file attributes, refer to the
                           ATTRIB command in *Part Four* for
                           details. This command is available only
                           when the File Display window is active.

COPY
(**F8** function key)

Copies selected files to a new drive or directory when the File Display window is active. Also, this menu command can be used to copy program items to a new program window if the Task Swapper is enabled and the Program window is active.

CREATE

Adds new subdirectories below the current directory. This command is available only when the Directory Tree window is active.

DELETE (Del)

Removes selected files from the disk when the File Display window is active. Also, this menu command can be used to delete a program item in the current program window if the Task Swapper is enabled and the Program window is active.

DESELECT ALL

Deselects all the highlighted files in the currently logged directory. This command is available only when the File Display window is active.

EXIT (Alt-F4)

Leaves the DOS shell and returns to the command prompt.

MOVE
(**F7** function key)

Changes the directory location of specified files when the File Display window is active.

NEW

Adds a program item to the current program group or nests a new program group window below the current one, when the Program window is active. Refer to *The Program Window* section in *Part Three* for details. Also, if the Active Task List window is active, this command appears on the File menu, but has no effect.

OPEN (Enter)

Opens files and applications. This command opens highlighted files when the File Display window is active. The Open command will start an application that has been previously associated with a data file using the Associate command. If an executable file is highlighted, the Open command will launch the application.

This command opens program groups or program items when the Program window is active. If a program group is highlighted, the Open command will activate it and display its contents in the program window area. If a program item is highlighted, the Open command will invoke its associated command.

If the Active Task List window is active, this command launches the highlighted task. If the Directory Tree window is active, this command appears on the File menu but has no effect.

PRINT

Sends the contents of a data file to the printer. The Print command is available only if you have initialized the DOS printing queue before entering the shell and the File Display window is active. Refer to the PRINT command in *Part Four* for details on initializing the printing queue.

PROPERTIES

Modifies the configuration of program groups and windows. This command is available only when the Program window is active. Refer to *The Program Window* section in *Part Three* for details.

RENAME	Prompts you to change the names of highlighted files when the File Display window is active, or directories when the Directory Tree window is active.
REORDER	Changes the order of display of program groups and items in the Program window. This command is available only when the Program window is active.
RUN	Runs any executable file or DOS line command from a dialog box.
SEARCH	Looks for files on the currently logged drive when the File Display window is active. Wildcard characters are allowed; useful if you would like to search for a group of related files. Looks for directories when the Directory Tree window is active.
SELECT ALL (**Ctrl-/**)	Selects and highlights all the files in the currently logged directory. This command is available only when the File Display window is active.
VIEW FILE CONTENTS (**F9** function key)	Displays the contents of data files. This command is available only when the File Display window is active.

A separate menu bar appears while the file is displayed. Pick the Display keyword to activate a pull-down menu that allows you to display the file in ASCII or hexadecimal formats. Alternatively, you may switch between formats by pressing **F9**. Pick the View keyword to activate a pull-down menu that offers you two choices: You can select Repaint the Screen, in case scrolling the file display does not update your screen properly (you can also accomplish this by pressing **Shift-F5**); or you can select Restore View, which returns you to the original shell display (you can also accomplish this by pressing **Esc**). The Help keyword activates the standard Help pull-down menu.

You cannot modify files that are displayed using this command.

OPTIONS MENU COMMANDS

This section lists the commands that appear when you select the Options keyword in the menu bar. These commands configure certain fundamental aspects of the shell's screen display and control how files are displayed and selected in the File Display window. For more details on individual commands, highlight the command in the menu and press the **F1** function key.

COLORS
Controls the color configuration of the shell display.

CONFIRMATION
Controls the display of confirmation prompts before deleting or overwriting files. You can control confirmation on the following functions:

Confirm on Delete — Displays a dialog box asking you to confirm before any file is deleted.

Confirm on Replace — Displays a dialog box asking you to confirm before any file is overwritten.

Confirm on Mouse Operation — Displays a dialog box asking you to confirm whenever a mouse operation is about to cause a file to be deleted or overwritten; for example, when moving a file from one directory to another containing a file of the same name.

DISPLAY

Controls the shell resolution and icon display. The Display command allows you to choose between *text mode,* which displays only ASCII characters and does not include icons, and *graphics mode,* which permits various graphic character display, including icons. If your system is not capable of graphics display, you cannot select graphics mode options; use text mode instead. In addition to choosing the mode, you can choose the number of lines that the shell displays on a single screen.

ENABLE TASK SWAPPER

Enables or disables support for multiple programs to remain in RAM, saving you the time it takes to exit and reload them. This command is available only when the Directory Tree or File Display window is active, and there are no currently active tasks in the Active Task List window. Refer to the *Task Swapping* section in *Part Three* for details.

FILE DISPLAY OPTIONS

Controls the included file types and listing order of file names in the File Display window.

SELECT ACROSS DIRECTORIES

Controls whether multiple files may be selected in more than one directory.

SHOW INFORMATION

Displays a dialog box containing file and disk statistics. This command is available only when the File Display or Directory Tree window is active.

VIEW MENU COMMANDS

This section describes the commands that appear when you select the View keyword in the menu bar. These commands help manage the configuration of the shell's various windows. To change the display, simply select one of the menu options discussed in this section. For more details on individual commands, highlight the command in the menu and press the **F1** function key.

ALL FILES

Displays the File Display window only, with file, directory, and drive information for the currently highlighted file on the left. This option does not display the Directory Tree, Program, or Active Task List windows. Task swapping is permitted using file names to launch applications and shortcut keys to move between them.

DUAL FILE LISTS

Displays two sets of Drive Display, Directory Tree, and File Display windows, one above the other. This configuration is useful for more sophisticated file management tasks and for using the mouse to move and copy files between drives.

PROGRAM LIST

Displays only the Program window, plus the Active Task List window when the Task Swapping feature is enabled. This configuration is good when you are using the shell strictly as an application manager, not as a file manager.

PROGRAM/FILE LIST

Displays all windows: Directory Tree, File Display, Program, and Active Task List (when the Task Swapping feature is enabled). Allows you to launch applications by selecting program items and file names from the Active Task List. This configuration is the default.

REFRESH
(**F5** function key)

Updates the file directory screen. This may become necessary from time to time because commands that are invoked within the shell operate within a secondary command processor. If these commands add or delete files or directories, the changes may not be reflected in the display windows when you return to the shell. Invoke this command (or press F5) to make the file and directory displays current. This command is available only when the Directory Tree or File Display window is active.

REPAINT SCREEN
(**Shift-F5** function key)

Repaint Screen redraws the shell window display if the display has been marred or otherwise altered by DOS commands, dialog boxes, or applications.

SINGLE FILE LIST   This option displays the Drive Letter Display, the Directory Tree window, and the File Display window, but does not display the Program window or the Active Task List window. When the Task Swapper is enabled, you may launch multiple applications by clicking on application file names or data file names associated with applications and switch between them using shortcut keys. For details on multiple applications, refer to the *Task Swapping* section in *Part Three*. This configuration is more useful when you are using the shell almost exclusively as a file manager, not a program manager.

TREE MENU COMMANDS

This section describes the commands that appear when you select the Tree keyword in the menu bar. These commands change the display of the Directory Tree, and are available only when the Directory Tree or File Display window is active. To change the directory display, simply pick one of the menu options discussed in this section. For more details on individual commands, highlight the command in the menu and press the **F1** function key.

COLLAPSE BRANCH (–)   Hides the display of subdirectories nested below the highlighted directory.

EXPAND ALL (Ctrl+*)   Reveals the entire directory
                              structure of the currently
                              logged drive. This command is
                              available only if the entire
                              directory structure is not
                              already displayed.

EXPAND BRANCH (*)   Reveals all subdirectories, if
                              any, nested below the
                              highlighted directory. This
                              command is available only if
                              all the nested subdirectories are
                              not already displayed.

EXPAND ONE LEVEL (+)   Reveals subdirectories, if any,
                              nested one level below the
                              highlighted directory.

Part Four

DOS Commands

This section contains a quick reference to all the DOS line commands for version 6.0, along with examples of their use. Whether you are looking up a particular command or just browsing around, the best way to get a feel for these commands is to read the description of their syntax, then try entering the examples at the DOS prompt. In some cases, you may need to substitute your own system's drive letters, subdirectories, and file names for those used in the examples. Do experiment with variations on the examples you see here, but only after you have made complete, reliable backup copies of your data; that way, if you make a mistake, you can restore data using your backup copy and try another approach without difficulty.

APPEND

Establishes a subdirectory search path for data files. When a data search path is set using APPEND, DOS will look in the currently logged subdirectory first, followed by the subdirectories in the search path.

• SYNTAX

First usage:

APPEND /E or /X

Subsequent usage:

APPEND *source:\path ;additional drive(s):\path(s) /switches*

You may need to invoke APPEND twice: first to set the environment switches (see in the Options section); second to specify the subdirectory search path for data files. Do not attempt to use the /E option at the same time you indicate the data search path.

You may name any number of subdirectories in the search path, but you are limited to 127 characters total (including 7 for the APPEND command and a space). Each subdirectory in the search path must be named separately; nested subdirectories are not included automatically. Type a semicolon between each name in the search path.

If you invoke APPEND without parameters, it will display the current data search path.

● SWITCHES

/E	Stores the search path within the DOS environment space, in a variable named APPEND. The environment space must be large enough to accommodate the search path; refer to *Appendix B* for details on adjusting the environment space. This parameter is legal only the first time you invoke APPEND, before you use APPEND again to establish the search path.
/X:on	Allows executable files (*.EXE, *.COM) to access the data search path. Using /X is the same as using /X:on. You can use this parameter any time when using APPEND.
/X:off	Cancels the ability of additional DOS external commands (such as FIND) to use the data search path.
/path:on	Uses the data search path whether or not data file names include drive letters or subdirectories.
/path:off	Does not use the data search path if data file names include drive letters or subdirectories.
; (semicolon)	Cancels the current data search path.

● EXAMPLES

APPEND /E /X

places the data search path in the DOS environment space, rather than in normal RAM, and indicates that other commands will use the data search path.

APPEND C:\WORD;\WPDATA

instructs DOS to look for data files on the C:\WORD subdirectory, and the \WPDATA subdirectory on the currently logged drive.

APPEND C:\WORD /path:off

instructs DOS to look for data files on the C:\WORD subdirectory, except for data files that already include a drive letter and/or a subdirectory path name.

    APPEND ;

cancels the current data file search path.

● **NOTES**   Some application software may not be written to take advantage of the data search path. For example, many word processors can open a file in the search path, but when saving the file, they will not overwrite the original file. Instead, they will create a new file with the same name in the default subdirectory.

Do not use APPEND with Windows.

APPEND is intended for use with data files. Use PATH to establish a search path for executable program files. DOS will look for program files if you have specified the /X:on parameter. When /X:on is specified, DOS looks for program files in the following order: the current directory, the appended directories, and then the search path.

APPEND is a natural choice for inclusion in AUTOEXEC.BAT, as it establishes a data search path at boot time.

You can use the APPEND command to establish a search path on network drives.

See Also   PATH

ATTRIB

Changes or displays the attributes of a file. Files can be declared read-only, read-write, archived, or not archived. As of version 5.0, hidden and system files may also be declared. In DOS 6, attributes of directories may be changed.

● SYNTAX

ATTRIB *modes target drive:\path\file(s) /switches*

ATTRIB requires a file name parameter. The file name may contain wildcard characters. If called without parameters, ATTRIB will display the attributes of all files matching the indicated file name.

● SWITCHES

/S   Used with file names that contain wildcard characters or subdirectory names without file names. This option will include matching files in subdirectories nested below the current subdirectory.

You cannot use more than one mode option at a time. The following mode options are used by ATTRIB:

+R   Changes specified file(s) to read-only, which means the file(s) cannot be overwritten or erased

−R   Changes specified file(s) to read-write, which means the files may be overwritten or erased

+A   Changes file setting(s) to Archived

−A   Changes file setting(s) to Not Archived

+H   Changes specified file(s) to hidden, which means the file(s) will not be visible to most DOS operations.

−H   Makes hidden file(s) visible again.

+S   Marks specified file(s) as DOS system file(s).

−S   Removes DOS system-file setting.

● EXAMPLES

ATTRIB ATTRIB.EXE

will display the attributes of the file ATTRIB.EXE.

ATTRIB +R C:\DOS*.* /S

will change all the files on the C:\DOS subdirectory, and any sub-directories nested below \DOS, to read-only.

● **NOTES**   Setting a file attribute to read-only is a good way to prevent its accidental erasure. Many files with the extensions .COM or .EXE can be set to read-only without problems. If you are on a network, you may be required to do this. In some cases, an application's attempt to overwrite a read-only file may generate an error message.

The setting of the Archive bit affects the behavior of other DOS commands. The RESTORE command will not copy archived files if the /M option is used. XCOPY will copy only archived files if the /A or /M options are used.

To use ATTRIB to change or display the attributes of a directory, you must specify a single directory name. Do not use wildcards with directories.

BREAK

Determines when the computer checks to see if Ctrl-C, which cancels most DOS commands, was entered by the user.

● **SYNTAX**

BREAK *ON or OFF*

BREAK may be invoked with either the ON or OFF parameter. If you invoke BREAK OFF, DOS checks to see if the user entered Ctrl-C during processes that update the screen, write characters to the printer, or read the keyboard buffer. If you invoke BREAK ON, DOS also checks for Ctrl-C during additional functions such as disk reading and writing. More frequent checking for Ctrl-C can cause some slowdown in overall performance during disk reading and writing.

BREAK OFF is the default state when you first boot up. You can invoke the BREAK=ON command in CONFIG.SYS.

If you enter BREAK without parameters, DOS reports the current BREAK status.

• EXAMPLE

BREAK ON

most frequently checks for Ctrl-C from the user.

CD OR CHDIR

Displays or changes the currently logged subdirectory.

• SYNTAX

CD *drive:\path* ..

CHDIR *drive:\path* ..

The CD command is a short version of the CHDIR command; they both do the same thing.

If you invoke the CD command with the name of a valid subdirectory on the current drive, DOS logs that subdirectory as the default. If you include a drive letter that is not the current drive, DOS logs the subdirectory on the specified drive as the default, but does not change the currently logged drive and path.

If you invoke CD without options, DOS displays the currently logged subdirectory.

You can log onto a subdirectory that is nested on the next deeper level by invoking CD followed by the subdirectory name.

• SWITCH

..   Logs onto the subdirectory nested just above the current one, if any

• EXAMPLES

The following sequence of commands assumes that your drive contains a subdirectory path \DOS\TEXT.

    CD \DOS\TEXT

logs the \DOS\TEXT subdirectory as the default on the current drive.

    CD ..

logs onto the \DOS subdirectory, which is one level above \DOS\TEXT.

    CD TEXT

logs back down to the \DOS\TEXT subdirectory if you are in the \DOS subdirectory.

    CD

displays *C:\DOS\TEXT*.

• NOTE   You can change the default directory on a drive other than the current one by specifying the drive letter before the directory name. This changes only the default on the other directory; you will remain logged onto your current drive and directory.

See Also   MKDIR, MD

CHCP

Changes or displays the current *code page*, which contains a language-specific character set used by DOS.

● SYNTAX

CHCP *code page number*

CHCP may be used to change the current code page by indicating a number corresponding to a valid code page set stored in the system, using the COUNTRY command in CONFIG.SYS. Here are examples of valid code page numbers:

437	United States
850	Multilingual
852	Slavic
860	Portuguese
863	Canadian-French
865	Nordic

CHCP invoked without options displays the currently active code page.

Only one code page may be active at any one time, although you may prepare as many as you need.

● EXAMPLES

CHCP

displays the current code page (437 on most U.S. systems).

CHCP 863

changes the code page to the Canadian-French symbol set, provided that set is prepared for use by your system.

● **NOTES**   Code pages are the means by which DOS supports multiple languages. A code page table defines a set of 256 characters specific to a country or language. The characters are translated from the code page table and displayed on the screen. In order to use an alternate code page, you must first prepare the code page table for use by your system.

Before using this command, be sure you have included the COUNTRY command in the CONFIG.SYS file. This command specifies the location of the file COUNTRY.SYS.

Prepare the code page by first invoking the NLSFUNC command. If you have installed device drivers with your system (using the DEVICE command in CONFIG.SYS), use the MODE CODEPAGE PREPARE command to prepare the desired code page for your device.

Refer also to the commands NLSFUNC and MODE, and the COUNTRY command in *Appendix A*. Once you have prepared code page tables, you may use CHCP to switch between them.

See Also   COUNTRY, NLSFUNC, MODE

CHKDSK

Can overwrite or erase data!

Analyzes, diagnoses, and optionally corrects common hard-disk errors. Reports on the status of files on disk.

● SYNTAX

CHKDSK *drive:\path\file(s) /switches*

If you invoke CHKDSK without parameters, DOS will analyze the current default disk. If you invoke CHKDSK followed by another drive letter, CHKDSK will analyze that drive.

Alternatively, you may specify a file name, including a full sub-directory path if not the currently logged one. Wildcard characters are allowed in file names. In this case, CHKDSK will check the disk and report on whether the specified files are *contiguous* (stored in adjacent areas of the disk) or *noncontiguous* (scattered over separate areas of the disk). Although there is no harm in noncontiguous files, a large number of widely scattered files can noticeably slow down your computer's performance. Refer to the DEFRAG command for more information.

● USING CHKDSK   CHKDSK examines the hard disk and
reports certain common errors. The most common errors found by CHKDSK are *lost clusters*, *cross-linking*, and *allocation errors*.

A lost cluster is an area of disk marked as unusable because it is supposedly occupied by a file, even though DOS can find no file name allocated to that area. Lost clusters normally develop when application programs that write temporary files to disk are inter-rupted before they can erase these files. Lost clusters are not serious, but they do waste hard-disk space and should be corrected; refer to the /F option in the Options section for details.

Cross-linking occurs when DOS finds more than one file name allo-cated to the same area of the hard disk. This means that one or all of the files in question are suspect. To correct a cross- linking condi-tion, do the following:

- If the files are data files, back them up onto blank, for-matted floppy disks. Do not use any existing backup disks, as you run the risk of overwriting good data with bad. Examine the files on the floppy disk to determine which ones are damaged. Erase the files on the hard disk and, if possible, replace them with verified backups.

- If any of the cross-linked files are executable program files, erase them and replace them using your master backup disks. Do not simply copy the backup files onto the hard disk, as this may not alleviate the cross-linked condition. Erase the files on the hard disk first, then copy the backups.

File allocation errors occur when the record of hard-disk space allocated to the files is inconsistent, impossible, or unreadable for any reason. CHKDSK will attempt to correct the problem if you have specified the /F option, but it may not be able to do so. If a file is damaged because of allocation errors, erase it and replace it from your backup disk.

After damaged files are replaced, run CHKDSK again to verify that the problem is solved.

Cross-linking and file allocation errors can be temporary problems (the result of power surges and spikes, for example) or they can be symptoms of more serious hardware problems. If these problems persist, have your computer checked by a qualified service technician.

● SWITCHES

/F   Enables auto-correction mechanism. When lost clusters are found, this message is displayed:

> ### *nn* lost clusters found in *n* chains
>
> ### Convert lost clusters to files (Y/N)?

where *n* is a number indicating the quantities involved. If you answer Y, the lost clusters are converted to files, giving them the name FILE*nnnn*.CHK, where *nnnn* is a number from 0000 to 9999. You can review, edit, rename, or delete these files as you wish. If you answer N, the lost clusters are simply removed.

/V   Displays the name of each file on disk as it checks. Because hard disks can contain hundreds of files, this option will often produce a long report. You may wish to redirect the report to a file.

• EXAMPLES

CHKDSK /F

checks the current hard disk and attempts to fix any errors it finds.

CHKDSK D:\DOS*.* /V > D:\STATUS.FIL

checks the files on the D:\DOS subdirectory, displays the name of all the files on disk, and redirects the output to a file named D:\STATUS.FIL.

• **NOTES**   CHKDSK reports logical errors in the file allocation table and directories. It does not check for errors in the files.

Because CHKDSK's automatic error-correction mechanism can overwrite information you may not want to lose, it is advisable to run it twice: the first time without the /F option to determine if cross-linking or allocation errors exist that would be better to correct manually, and the second time with the /F option to automatically erase lost clusters or fix other errors.

If you redirect CHKDSK's disk status report to a file, do not use the /F parameter.

Do not run CHKDSK/F from inside other applications, even those that allow you to access the DOS prompt. Many applications create temporary files while running, and CHKDSK can mistakenly report these files as errors. If you attempt to make corrections, you risk damaging your data.

For this reason, do not attempt to use CHKDSK within Windows, while running the TASK swapper in the DOS Shell, or across a network. Do not use CHKDSK on drives that have been renamed with the SUBST command.

CLS

Clears the screen.

● SYNTAX

CLS

The CLS command is invoked without parameters. It will erase all characters on the screen and display the operating system prompt, if any, on the first line of the display.

● NOTE
If your display is configured for more than 25 lines, CLS may not clear it properly. Check the documentation for your display device for alternatives to CLS.

COMMAND

Invokes a secondary command processor.

● SYNTAX

COMMAND *drive:\path device /switches*

COMMAND called without parameters starts a new command processor in front of the currently loaded one. This secondary command processor includes the parent processor's environment settings. If you change settings in the secondary processor, they are lost when you return to the parent processor. To return to the parent processor, invoke the EXIT command.

You can nest additional secondary processors, but available RAM is reduced slightly for each one.

If you include the source drive and path parameters, the new command processor will look for the file COMMAND.COM on that subdirectory as needed; otherwise it looks for COMMAND.COM in the same location as the primary processor.

You may specify an auxiliary device parameter (such as COM1, for connection to a remote terminal). The effect of this parameter is the same as invoking the CTTY command in the secondary processor.

● SWITCHES

/E:*nnnnn*

Creates a new environment size for variables. (See the SET entry for details regarding DOS variables.) The range for a valid environment size is 160 to 32,768 bytes.

/K:*file*

Runs the executable program or batch file specified by *file* and then displays the MS-DOS command prompt. Use this switch when you are starting a secondary processor and want to specify an automatic file other than AUTOEXEC.BAT. Microsoft does not recommend that use of this switch in CONFIG.SYS. Use AUTOEXEC.BAT at boot time.

/P

Allows the secondary command processor to function as the primary processor. DOS will not automatically return to the parent processor. This switch is generally used only in the CONFIG.SYS file, when first starting the system.

/C *command string*

Invokes a DOS command or executable file and returns to the parent processor immediately upon completion (unless the /P switch has also been invoked).

/MSG[*]   Loads all DOS error messages into memory. Use this option when running DOS on a floppy-disk based system where you are switching disks frequently. You must use the /P option with this option.

● EXAMPLES

COMMAND

loads the secondary processor and displays the current version of DOS.

COMMAND /P /E:1024

loads the secondary processor, indicates that it is to be treated as the primary processor, and enlarges the DOS environment space to 1024 bytes. This is the only way to enlarge the environment size in DOS versions prior to 3.3.

COMMAND /C MY-PROG

loads the secondary processor, executes the batch file MY-PROG.BAT, and returns to the parent processor at the conclusion of MY-PROG. In DOS versions prior to 3.3, this is the only method for calling an additional batch file from within a batch file and then returning to the original batch file afterwards. Although commonly used with batch files, this syntax will function the same way for any executable file.

● **NOTES** Secondary command processors are normally used by application software to create a new DOS environment (called a *shell*) while the original application is still running, for purposes of executing file management commands or additional applications. In versions of DOS prior to 3.3, COMMAND was used to execute batch files from within other batch files, and then return to the original upon completion.

Do not load TSR (terminate-and-stay-resident) programs, such as SIDEKICK, or run any program that makes lasting changes to the organization of RAM, while within a secondary processor. These types of programs may cause unpredictable results when you return to the parent processor, and may lead to the loss of data. Especially avoid loading programs from within application software (spreadsheets, word processors, and so on) that allow you to access the DOS prompt without leaving the program. TSR programs installed in this manner can conflict with the application's organization of RAM. If you intend to use a TSR program, load it while in the primary processor, then create the secondary processor.

See Also EXIT, CALL

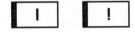

Can overwrite or erase data!

Copies and combines files.

● SYNTAX

COPY *source:\path\file(s) target:\path\file(s) /switches*

Alternative syntax for combining files:

COPY *source file(s)+source file(s)+ ... target\path\file(s) /switches*

At a minimum, the COPY command requires a *source file name*, which may include wildcard characters, plus optional drive letter and subdirectory path. Optionally you may provide a target parameter, which may be another file name, drive letter, or subdirectory path, or a combination of the three. If you do not include a target, COPY will attempt to copy the source files onto the currently logged drive and subdirectory.

The source and target may not indicate the same file name in the same location. In other words, the COPY command will not copy a file onto itself.

If the target is a drive or a directory but does not include a file name, a copy with the same name as the source file is made in the target location. If you indicate subdirectories, they must be preceded by a backslash (\) character.

If you use wildcard characters to indicate multiple source files and the target does not include a file name, a set of individual copies of each file matching the source specification will be made in the target location.

If you indicate multiple source files and the target file name also includes wildcard characters, DOS will attempt to rename the target files in accordance with the wildcard conventions that you indicate. For predictable results, keep the wildcard character specifications consistent between the source and target file names.

If you indicate multiple source files and the target is a single file name, DOS will combine the source files matching the wildcard specification into the single target file.

Alternatively, you may combine files by listing source files, separating them with a plus sign (+). These source files may include wildcard characters as well. The files will be combined into the file you indicate as the target file. It is inadvisable to combine files if one of the source files has the same name as the target. However, you may omit a target file name, and DOS will combine the source files into a file with the same name as the first source file, thereby overwriting it.

• SWITCHES

/A Indicates that the files are to be treated as ASCII files. The location of this switch in the command line is important. It affects the file name immediately preceding it, plus all file names that follow it until another /A or /B switch is encountered. When a file is treated as an ASCII file, it is read until a Ctrl-Z (end-of-file) character is encountered or until DOS has read the maximum number of bytes as specified in the file directory. If this switch is used after the target file name, a Ctrl-Z character will be added to the end of the target file. This switch is the default when combining files.

/B Indicates that the files are to be treated as binary files. As with the /A switch, the location of this switch in the command line is important. It affects the file name immediately preceding it, plus all file names that follow it until another /A or /B switch is encountered. When a file is treated as a binary file, DOS will continue reading when a Ctrl-Z character is encountered, to the reported size of the file. If this switch is used after the target file name, a Ctrl-Z character will not be added to the end of the target file. This switch is the default unless you are combining files or copying to a device.

/V Instructs DOS to perform a validity check on the target files after they are created. The extra step of verification will slow COPY down slightly. The same effect can be made default with the command VERIFY ON.

• EXAMPLES

COPY /B *.* A:

copies all files on the currently logged drive and subdirectory to drive A. DOS ignores end-of-file characters. Remember to include the colon after the drive letter. If you forget, all the files on the currently logged drive and subdirectory will be copied into one file named A.

COPY /A *.TXT *.BAK /A /V

copies all files with extension .TXT to files with the same name and extension .BAK. DOS honors end-of-file characters in all files, appends an end-of-file character on each new file it creates, and verifies the copies that are made.

COPY /B *.TXT \BACKUP /V

copies all files with extension .TXT to a subdirectory named BACK-UP on the same logged drive. All files are treated as binary files, and DOS verifies the copies that are made.

COPY A:*.TXT

copies all files on drive A with the extension .TXT to the currently logged drive and subdirectory. The currently logged drive must not be drive A.

COPY START.FIL + MIDDLE.FIL + END.FIL COMPLETE.FIL

combines START.FIL, MIDDLE.FIL, and END.FIL into one file called COMPLETE.FIL.

COPY REPORT.TXT + *.TXT

copies all files with extension .TXT, except REPORT.TXT, into RE-PORT.TXT. DOS honors REPORT.TXT as the target file name because it is the first name on the list of files to combine. However, notice that the wildcard specification, *.TXT, would include REPORT.TXT. DOS cannot honor the instruction to combine REPORT.TXT with itself; thus the contents of REPORT.TXT are not duplicated in the resulting file.

COPY /A LETTER.TXT PRN

copies a file to the standard printing device. Be sure your printing device is online, or DOS will simply wait, not accepting any further input. In addition to PRN, you may also copy files to the device names COM1, COM2, COM3, COM4, AUX, CON, LPT1, or LPT2. Not all systems support all of these device names. If your system does not support the device name, DOS will create a disk file with that name.

● **NOTES**   The /A switch, which adds an end-of-file marker to the destination file, is designed for special circumstances in which some older applications may require an end-of-file marker in files that they read.

The /B switch is designed for circumstances in which binary information may be lost or misinterpreted; for example, if you are using the COPY command to send downloadable soft fonts to your printer.

The /V switch compares the contents of the target file on a sector-by-sector basis to an image of the file in RAM, not to the actual source file on disk. Thus, this switch will detect errors writing the target file, but can miss errors that may occur reading the source file into RAM.

For everyday purposes of making copies of files on disk, most files will copy just fine without the use of any of COPY's optional switches. The general rule is this: If you don't really need them, don't use them.

You can use the COPY command to attach the current time and date to a file without changing it, using a pair of commas as the target parameter:

COPY *file*+,,

Use this command with the exact name of one file only. Do not use wildcards to change a group of files.

See Also   XCOPY

Redirects console input and output to a named hardware device. When console input and output is redirected, the computer can operate on instructions and display messages using a remote input/output device.

• SYNTAX

CTTY *device name*

CTTY requires a valid hardware device name. Common secondary device names include CON (default console); PRN, LPT1, LPT2, LPT3, (printer ports); COM1, COM2, COM3, and COM4 (serial communications ports); and AUX, (another terminal connected to the computer).

• EXAMPLES

CTTY COM1

instructs DOS to handle subsequent input and output through the COM1 communications port.

CTTY CON

redirects input and output functions through the default device (usually the keyboard and monitor). This command must be sent from whatever input device is current, for example, a remote terminal connected via a *COM* port.

• NOTES   Applications that do not use DOS for input and output (that is, they have their own internal instructions for sending and receiving data) will not honor any redirection made using CTTY. Use the MODE command to set up your serial port before using CTTY. You also can use the *device* parameter of the COMMAND command to specify the input device.

Even if you redirect input and output using CTTY, you can still reboot the computer with Ctrl-Alt-Del from the default system keyboard.

See Also   MODE, COMMAND

DATE

Displays or sets the system date.

● SYNTAX

DATE *date*

If you invoke the DATE command without parameters, DOS displays the current system date and prompts you to enter another. Dates are accepted using the format *mm/dd/yy*, where *mm* is the month (1–12), *dd* is the day (1–31), and *yy* is the year from 1980 to 2079 (80–79).

Some alternate formats are accepted. You may use hyphens (–) rather than slashes (/) to separate the month, day, and year. You may also use 4 digits for the year (1980–2079).

Date formats used in other countries are accepted if you have changed the code page to another character set, using the COUNTRY command in CONFIG.SYS. See *Appendix A* for details.

If you include the date in an accepted format on the command line, DOS changes the date without displaying a message.

● EXAMPLES

DATE

displays the current date and prompts you to enter another. To leave the date unchanged, press Enter.

DATE 10-26-93

changes the date to October 26, 1993.

● **NOTES**   DOS maintains a system date even if your computer does not have an internal clock.

If your computer has an internal clock, the DATE command will reset it. If you do not use an AUTOEXEC.BAT file, DOS invokes the DATE command automatically at startup. If you are using AUTOEXEC.BAT, you must include the DATE command in the file to achieve the same effect.

See Also   TIME

DBLSPACE

Manages compressed data disks.

● SYNTAX

   DBLSPACE */switches drive:*

The first time you invoke DBLSPACE, it runs through an automatic self-configuration routine. It compresses the data on a drive that you select, usually drive C. The process takes a significant amount of time. During the process, DBLSPACE re-starts your computer twice. Refer to *Part Two* for more details on setting up DBLSPACE and compressed drives.

Compressed data drives appear to function just like uncompressed drives; the process of handling compressed data is completely transparent to the user.

After DBLSPACE has configured itself, you can invoke the DBLSPACE command to manage certain functions of your compressed drive.

● SWITCHES

drive:	Displays information about a drive
/CHKDSK *drive:*	Checks a compressed disk for errors on *drive*. If no errors are found, no message is displayed.
/CHKDSK /F *drive:*	Fixes errors on compressed *drive*.
/COMPRESS *drive:*	Compress an existing *drive*.
/COMPRESS /NEWDRIVE=*new: drive:*	Compress an existing drive where *new:* is a new drive letter and *drive:* is the drive letter of the existing drive.
/CONVSTAC=*stacvol*	Convert a Stacker volume where *stacvol* is the name of the Stacker volume to convert.
/CONVSTAC=*stacvol* /NEWDRIVE=*new:*	Convert a Stacker volume where *stacvol* is the name of the Stacker volume to convert, and *new:* is a new drive letter for the converted volume.
/CONVSTAC=*stacvol* /CVF=*nnn:*	Convert a Stacker volume where *stacvol* is the name of the Stacker volume to convert and *nnn* is a new Converted Volume File number.
/CREATE *drive:*	Create a new compressed *drive*.
/CREATE /NEWDRIVE=*new: drive:*	Create a new compressed where *new:* is a new drive letter and *drive* is the existing standard drive.

/CREATE /SIZE=*n.nn drive:*	Create a new compressed drive where *n.nn* is the new size and *drive* is an existing standard drive.
/DEFRAGMENT *drive:*	Rewrite files on the compressed *drive* in contiguous sectors.
/DELETE *drive:*	Delete compressed *drive*. All files are lost.
/FORMAT *drive:*	Reformat compressed *drive*. All files are lost.
/MAP	Display the characteristics of all drives.
/MAXCOMPRESS *drive:*	Allows increased compression of *drive*.
/MOUNT=*nnn drive:*	Connects a compressed volume to drive letter *drive*, where *nnn* is the number of the compressed volume file.
/MOUNT=*nnn* /NEWDRIVE=*new: drive:*	Connects a compressed volume to drive letter *drive*, and assigns new drive letter *new*. *nnn* is the number of the compressed volume file.
/RATIO=*n.nn drive:*	Assigns a new compression ratio to compressed *drive*.
/SIZE=*n.nn drive:*	Changes the size of *drive*, where *n.nn* is the new drive size.
/UNMOUNT *drive:*	Disconnects *drive* from its compressed volume file.

• EXAMPLES

DBLSPACE /COMPRESS D:

changes existing disk D: to a compressed drive, using default size and compression ratio.

    DBLSPACE /MOUNT=001 /A:

connects the compressed floppy drive in A: to compressed volume 001.

    DBLSPACE /UNMOUNT A:

disconnects the compressed floppy drive in drive A.

● **NOTES**   Changing a drive's compression ratio does not affect how files are actually compressed; instead, it affect only DBL-SPACE's estimate of available disk space on compressed volumes.

DBLSPACE creates a new, uncompressed drive on your hard disk. This drive is always one letter higher than the highest storage drive on your system (RAM disks excluded). DBLSPACE uses this drive exclusively. For example, it stores completely incompressible files here. You should not attempt to modify the files on this drive. Most files on this drive are hidden. To see them, log onto the drive and invoke ATTRIB.

Files ending in three digits are your compressed volume file, beginning with 000 for your first compressed drive and increasing after that.

DEFRAG

 E   NEW

Speeds up disk performance by reorganizing files.

● **SYNTAX**

    DEFRAG *drive: /switches*

As you use your hard disk, files become *fragmented*. This means that they are broken into sections and scattered in disparate areas of the disk. DEFRAG optimizes disk performance by arranging these fragmented files in contiguous sectors. This makes file reading faster and saves wear and tear on a disk's moving parts.

If you invoke the DEFRAG command without the *drive:* parameter, you are presented with a full screen, menu-driven system. You can select the drive you want to optimize and specify various options. You can use a mouse or the keyboard to move between various menu options. If you are using the keyboard, you can move between menu items using the arrow keys and select items by pressing the spacebar. Alternatively, you can select items by holding down the Alt key and pressing the keyboard key that corresponds to the highlighted character in the screen menu item.

DEFRAG includes an extensive online help system. To access online help, press F1.

Alternatively, you can select the drive and options by entering the drive letter on the command line when you invoke DEFRAG, along with various control switches.

● SWITCHES

/F   Arranges defragmented files so that there are
                no empty spaces between them.

/U   Does not reallocate defragmented files.
                (Empty spaces may be left between them.)

/S:*order*   Sorts the files in their directories, according
                to the value of *order*, which can be one or
                more of the following characters:

> N = Alphabetically by name
> N- = Reverse-alphabetically by name
> (Z through A)
> E = Alphabetically by extension
> E- = Reverse-alphabetically by extension
> (Z through A)
> D = Date/time, ascending
> D- = Date/time, descending
> S = Size, smallest to largest
> S- = Size, largest to smallest

When you use more than one character, files
are sorted first according to the leftmost
characters, then characters to the right
determine the order within duplicates.

/B   Restart the computer after defragmentation.

/V   Verifies that the defragmented files match the
                original file image in memory.

/SKIPHIGH   Forces DEFRAG to run from conventional
                memory. (Upper memory is default, if
                available).

• EXAMPLE

DEFRAG C: /F /S:EDS

defragments files and sorts them on disk so that no empty spaces
fall between them, and arranges them in directories by extension,
within duplicate extensions by date and time, and when date and
time are the same, by size.

• ERRORLEVEL CODES

0 = Defragmentation completed successfully

1 = Internal error detected while running DEFRAG

2 = Disk too full (No free clusters)

3 = Operator interrupted comparison with Ctrl-C

4 = General Disk failure

5 = Errors found reading clusters

6 = Errors found writing clusters

7 = File Allocation error (Run Chkdsk /F)

8 = Memory error

9 = Insufficient RAM

• NOTES   Do not run DEFRAG on network or Interlnk drives,
and do not run the program from within Windows.

If you have previously installed FASTOPEN, run DEFRAG with /B
switch to reboot the computer and update file locations in memory.

DEL OR ERASE

Can erase data!

Deletes files.

● SYNTAX

DEL *drive:\path\file(s) /switches*

ERASE *drive:\path\file(s) /switches*

The DEL and ERASE commands function identically. All references in this section to the DEL command apply as well to the ERASE command.

DEL requires that you specify the name of a file to delete. Wildcard characters may be used to erase groups of files. You may also specify a drive letter and subdirectory path, if different from the currently logged path. If you specify a subdirectory path without file names, DOS assumes you want to delete all the files in the subdirectory.

If you use just a subdirectory path, or the wildcard specification *.* (meaning all the files on the current subdirectory), DOS prompts

All files in directory will be deleted! Are you sure (Y/N)?

If you really intend to delete all the files, enter Y in response to this prompt. If you enter N, the command is canceled.

• SWITCH

/P   Instructs DOS to display each file that matches the file
      name parameter and prompt, "Delete (Y/N)?" If you
      enter Y, the file is deleted. If you enter N, the file is left
      alone. This safety device can help prevent you from
      accidentally deleting files. It also allows you to delete
      files selectively from a group.

• EXAMPLES

DEL EXAMPLE.TXT

deletes the file EXAMPLE.TXT.

DEL *.BAK

deletes all files on the current subdirectory with the extension .BAK.

DEL A:\

deletes all files in the root directory on drive A. Prompts for confirmation first.

DEL C:\BACKUP*.BAK /P

displays each file on the C:\BACKUP subdirectory with the extension .BAK, and prompts for confirmation before deleting it:

name, Delete (Y/N)?

where *name* is the name of the file about to be deleted. To confirm, enter Y.

• NOTE   See the UNDELETE entry for details on recovering files
that have been accidentally erased. If you must recover a file that has
been accidentally deleted, do so as quickly as you can. If possible,
do not use the computer for any other operation until any accidentally deleted files have been recovered.

See Also   UNDELETE

DELTREE

Can erase data!

Removes a directory, including all its files and subdirectories.

● SYNTAX

DELTREE */switch drive:\path*

Use the DELTREE command to quickly remove an unwanted directory, plus all files on it, and all subdirectories nested below it, in a single command. The *drive* parameter is the letter of a disk drive, required only if the directory is not on the current drive. The *\path* parameter is required, naming the directory you intend to delete. When used without the /Y switch, DELTREE prompts you to confirm that you want to delete the entire directory. Enter Y to confirm or any other key to abort.

● SWITCH

/Y   Suppresses the prompt that asks you to confirm that you want to delete the directory.

● EXAMPLE

DELTREE C:\BYEBYE

prompts for confirmation and, if you enter Y, deletes the \BYEBYE directory and all files in it.

• **NOTES**   DELTREE has the potential to permanently destroy enormous amounts of data. Use it with great caution, if at all. DELTREE will delete hidden, system, and read-only files. Notice especially that DELTREE wipes out all nested subdirectories as well. Be especially cautious with DELTREE if you are using copy-protected software, as many of these applications make use of hidden, system, and read-only files. If you use DELTREE on a directory containing copy-protection files, the protected application may no longer work.

Wildcards are allowed. If you use wildcards, all directories plus all files matching the wildcard specification will be deleted.

You cannot delete the currently logged directory, but you can delete all files on it and nested subdirectories using this command.

See Also   RD, DEL

DIR

Displays a list of files in a directory.

• **SYNTAX**

   DIR *drive:\path\file(s) /switches*

If you invoke DIR without parameters, it will display a list of files in the currently logged drive and subdirectory.

You may specify a drive or subdirectory other than the current one by specifying it on the command line.

You may limit the files included in the directory list by indicating a file name. If the file name contains wildcard characters, only those files that match the specification will be included.

Unless you specify the /W option, DOS displays the list one file to a line, including the file name, extension, size in bytes, date, and time the file was created.

● SWITCHES

/P   Causes the list of files to pause each time the file list fills the screen during the display. Press any key to continue displaying files in this manner, until DOS reaches the end of the list.

/W   Causes only file names and extensions to be listed, in a wide format with as many as five file names per line

/S   Displays files in all subdirectories nested below the specified directory

/B   Displays file and directory names only

/L   Displays file names in lowercase (mimics UNIX)

/C   Displays the compression ratio (files on Dblspace-compressed drives) This switch has no effect when used with /W or /B.

/O:*order*   List files in sorted order, where *order* is a letter indicating the one of the following:

> C = By compression ratio, low to high
> D = Chronological order
> E = File extension, then by name
> G = Group files by subdirectories
> N = File name, then by extension
> S = File size

To reverse the selected order, place a hyphen (–) before the *order* parameter.

/A:*attrib*   Includes only those files with specified attributes, where *attrib* is a letter indicating the type of attribute to include in the listing:

> A = Files with archive bit set
> D = Directories only
> R = Files marked read-only
> H = Hidden files
> S = System files

To reverse the meaning of the attribute, precede the *attrib* letter with a hyphen (–); for example, –A would indicate include files *without* the archive bit set.

• EXAMPLES

DIR A:

lists all the files on drive A.

DIR C: /P/W

lists all the files on the currently logged subdirectory of drive C, in wide format (names only), and pauses the display each time the screen fills up with file names.

DIR /O:N /A:H

displays only hidden files in alphabetical order.

• NOTES   You may store a default set of DIR command switches in the DIRCMD environment variable. For example:

SET DIRCMD=/O:N

indicates that all future DIR command calls will be in alphabetical order by file name. If you would like to override the DIRCMD switch temporarily, include the parameter on the command line, preceded by a hyphen (–). For example:

DIR /O:-N

would override the example DIRCMD switch.

If you redirect the output of DIR using a pipe character, the temporary file created by the pipe parameter will appear in the directory listing. To prevent this, use the SET command to create an environment variable named TEMP before invoking DIR.

See Also   TREE

DISKCOMP

Compares the contents of two floppy disks on a track-by-track basis, reporting which track numbers are not identical.

● SYNTAX

DISKCOMP *source: target: /switches*

DISKCOMP requires that you enter a source drive. This drive must be a drive letter for a floppy-disk drive.

If you do not specify a second drive for comparison, DOS uses the current default drive for the second drive.

If the source drive and the second drive are the same, DOS first reads the floppy disk in the source drive, then prompts you to remove the disks and insert the second disk into the same drive. You may have to switch disks more than once to complete the comparison process.

● SWITCHES

/1   Instructs DISKCOMP to compare only the first side of each disk, even double-sided disks.

/8   Instructs DISKCOMP to compare only the first 8 sectors of each track, even if the tracks have 9 or 15 sectors.

● EXAMPLES

DISKCOMP A:

compares the disk in drive A with the disk in the currently logged
drive. If the current drive is drive A, DISKCOMP prompts you to
switch disks at various times during the comparison.

DISKCOMP A: B: /1/8

compares the disk in drive A with the disk in drive B. Compares
only the first side of each disk, and only the first 8 sectors of each
track.

● ERRORLEVEL CODES

0 = Disks are identical

1 = Disks are not identical

2 = Operator interrupted comparison with Ctrl-C

3 = Comparison interrupted by data errors or damaged disks

4 = Invalid drive letters, drive types, or syntax error

● **NOTES**   DISKCOMP will only compare floppy disks that are
the same size and data density. For example, you cannot compare a
5.25", 1.2Mb disk with a 5.25", 360K disk. You cannot compare hard
disks or RAM disks using DISKCOMP.

You cannot use DISKCOMP on drives that have been reassigned
using the SUBST command. You cannot use DISKCOMP to compare drives across a network.

You can compare the contents of different drive types using the FC
command to compare the files.

See Also   FC

DISKCOPY

Copies the contents of one floppy disk to another on a track-by-track basis.

● SYNTAX

DISKCOPY *source: target: /switches*

If the source drive and the target drive parameters are the same, DOS first reads the floppy disk in the source drive, then prompts you to remove the disks and insert the target disk into the same drive. You may have to switch disks more than once to complete the copy process.

If you are logged onto a floppy-disk drive and invoke DISKCOPY without parameters, DOS prompts you to insert the source and target diskettes into the drive, as required. If you do not specify a target drive, DOS uses the currently logged floppy-disk drive for the target drive.

If the target disk is unformatted, DISKCOPY will format the disk first. To do so, FORMAT.COM must be available to DOS, either on the currently logged drive or the DOS search path.

● SWITCHES

/1   Instructs DISKCOPY to copy only the first side of each disk, even double-sided disks.

/V   Instructs DISKCOPY to perform a validity check on the data copied to the target disk. This extra step slows the copying process somewhat.

● EXAMPLES

DISKCOPY A:

copies the disk in drive A onto the disk in the currently logged drive. If the current drive is drive A, DISKCOPY prompts you to switch disks at various times during the copy process.

DISKCOPY A: B: /1

copies the disk in drive A onto the disk in drive B. Copies only the first side of the source disk.

● ERRORLEVEL CODES

0 = Copy completed successfully

1 = Read or write error caused differences between source and target

2 = Operator interrupted copy with Ctrl-C

3 = Copy interrupted by data errors or damaged disks

4 = Invalid drive letters, drive types, insufficient RAM, or syntax error

● **NOTES**   DISKCOPY will only copy floppy disks that are the same size. For example, you cannot copy a 5.25", 1.2Mb floppy onto a 3.5", 1.44Mb floppy. You cannot copy hard disks or RAM disks using DISKCOPY.

You should use DISKCOPY only with disks that have the same data capacity. If the capacity of your source disk is different from an (unformatted) target disk, DISKCOPY may prompt:

TARGET media has lower capacity than SOURCE Continue anyway (Y/N)?

If you press Y, DISKCOPY attempts to format the target disk and copy the files.

You cannot use DISKCOPY on drives that have been reassigned using the SUBST command. You cannot use DISKCOPY to copy disks across a network.

You can copy the contents of one disk to another disk of a different size or density using the XCOPY or COPY commands. The target disk must be large enough to accommodate all the source files.

DOS will create a new volume serial number on the target disk. Otherwise, disks made using DISKCOPY are track-and-sector duplicates of each other. This means that if there is a data error on the source disk, it most likely will be copied onto the target disk as well. Likewise, fragmented files on the source disk will be identically fragmented on the target disk.

If your version of DOS supports XCOPY, you can use that command instead, which will eliminate or call attention to some data errors and put together fragmented files on the target drive, with no significant loss of copying speed.

See Also   COPY, XCOPY

DOSHELP

Implements an abbreviated in-line help system.

● SYNTAX

DOSHELP command

Alternate syntax:

command **/?**

DOSHELP displays a quick summary of DOS command options. It is less detailed that you would get from the HELP command.

● SWITCH

The DOSHELP command has no switches, but every DOS command honors the /? switch, which displays the same information as DOSHELP *command*.

• EXAMPLE

DOSHELP MEMMAKER

displays a short summary of options for the MEMMAKER command.

MEMMAKER /?

displays the same information as the previous example. This syntax is marginally faster.

See Also HELP

DOSKEY

Allows DOS to remember DOS commands, and permits the user to move the cursor along the command line, editing DOS commands before they are invoked.

• SYNTAX

DOSKEY *macro=commands* [*/options*]

• USING DOSKEY DOSKEY may be invoked without options. Once invoked, DOSKEY saves previously invoked DOS commands in a special buffer in RAM. The user may recall these previous commands by scrolling through the buffer. Pressing the up arrow scrolls backward, pressing the down arrow scrolls forward.

Any command on the command line may be edited by moving the cursor to the appropriate point and retyping the correct characters. In DOSKEY's normal default state, typed characters will overstrike existing characters on the command line. If the user presses the Insert key, typed characters are inserted in place on the command line. Pressing Insert a second time returns to overstrike mode. Pressing Enter restores the default mode.

Each time the user enters a command, the command is added to DOSKEY's command buffer. This includes duplicate commands and edited commands.

DOSKEY uses about 4K of RAM. This amount can increase if you specify a large buffer size as a command line option.

DOSKEY does not affect the standard DOS function keys, but it adds function keys of its own:

F7	Displays commands stored in memory, with their associated line numbers.
ALT-F7	Deletes all commands stored in memory.
F8	Searches memory for a command. Type the first few characters of the desired command and press F8.
F9	Prompts for a command line number and displays the associated command.
ALT-F10	Deletes all macro definitions.

The *macro* parameter is user-defined name assigned to a set of keystrokes that are played back when the user enters DOSKEY followed by the macro name. To define a macro, invoke DOSKEY followed by the macro name, an equals sign, and the keystrokes you want to record. Special characters have control meanings in a macro. They are:

$g	Redirects output to a device or a file. Equal to > on the command line.
gg	Appends output to a device or a file. Equal to >> on the command line.
$l	Redirects input to a device or a file. Equal to < on the command line.
$b	Redirects output to a command. Equal to	on the command line.
$t	Separates commands when you create a macro.

$$ Specifies the literal dollar-sign character ($).

$1–$9 Represents replaceable parameters in a macro. Similar to the %1 character in a batch program.

$* Wild-card replaceable parameter. Accepts everything added on the command line after you invoke DOSKEY and a macro name.

● SWITCHES

/INSERT Changes command line editing to Insert mode as the default. Press the Insert key to toggle between Insert and Overstrike mode.

/OVERSTRIKE Changes command line editing to Overstrike mode as the default. This is the default state if no options are used. Press the Insert key to toggle between Overstrike and Insert mode.

/REINSTALL Installs an additional copy of DOSKEY in RAM. Clears the current command buffer. Resets new options if specified on the command line. Each time DOSKEY is reinstalled, it takes up an additional 4K of RAM, plus whatever size you specify for the buffer.

/BUFSIZE=*nnnn* Specifies the size of the command buffer, where *nnnn* is the size in bytes. Default is 512 bytes. The buffer size may be changed only when first installing or reinstalling DOSKEY.

/HISTORY Displays all stored command lines.

/MACROS Displays all Doskey macros.

● EXAMPLES

DOSKEY

installs the DOSKEY buffer in RAM.

DOSKEY D=DIR $1: /O:N /P

defines a macro named D, which will display a directory of a specified drive, in alphabetical order, and permits entry of the drive letter without a colon.

D A

executes the macro after it has been defined as in the previous example.

DOSKEY /REINSTALL /BUFSIZE=1024

installs an additional copy of DOSKEY, clears the command line buffer, and enlarges it to 1K.

EDIT

Starts a full-screen text editor.

● SYNTAX

EDIT *drive:\path\file* /D

EDIT is a menu-driven text editor. While not as fully-featured as a commercial word processor, it is handy for editing batch files, CONFIG.SYS, and other ASCII text files used by the operating system.

If you invoke EDIT without parameters, the editor appears without a default open file. Alternatively, you may specify a file for EDIT to open when it loads.

EDIT will display files other than ASCII files, but they will probably not be readable, and editing non-ASCII files this way can be dangerous.

You can use the editor's menus to select files to edit, mark, move, and copy blocks of text, and perform other basic editing tasks. You can save the files back to disk under the original name, or as new files under new names. You can also print the files from the editor.

You can use a mouse or the keyboard to move between various menu options. If you are using the keyboard, you can move between menu items using the arrow keys and select items by pressing the spacebar. Alternatively, you can select items by holding down the Alt key and pressing the keyboard key that corresponds to the highlighted character in the screen menu item.

EDIT includes an online help system. To access online help, select the Help keyword from the top line of the opening menu, or press F1 or Alt-H.

● SWITCHES

/B	Forces black and white display. Use this switch if the Editor doesn't display properly on your monitor.
/G	Speed up screen display on CGA monitors.
/H	Alters line display for the current monitor. Use this option if the editor overlaps or does not fill the screen.
/NOHI	Corrects display on an 8-color monitors.

● EXAMPLE

EDIT MY-TEXT.FIL

starts the editor with MY-TEXT.FIL as the default. If the file doesn't already exist, the editor creates it.

● **NOTE** EDIT requires that QBASIC.EXE be in the same directory as the file EDIT.COM, in the currently-logged directory, or on the DOS search path.

EXIT

Returns control from a secondary processor to the parent processor, if one exists. Otherwise, EXIT has no effect.

● SYNTAX

EXIT

EXIT accepts no parameters or options. It will return control of the computer to a parent processor only if a secondary processor has been previously enabled with the COMMAND command. When EXIT returns control to the parent processor, all variables and environment settings changed by the secondary processor are lost; settings return to those of the parent processor.

For details regarding secondary and parent processors, see the COMMAND entry.

● NOTE It is not advisable to load terminate-and-stay-resident (TSR) software, such as DOSKEY or SIDEKICK, while a secondary processor is active. The changes in RAM may adversely affect the behavior of the parent processor. Some application programs allow you to access a DOS "shell" by loading a secondary processor while a portion of the application program remains active. Avoid loading TSR software under these circumstances.

See Also COMMAND

FASTOPEN

| E | | TSR |

Enhances system performance by storing the hard disk locations of previously opened files and subdirectories in RAM, in order to speed up subsequent access of the same files and subdirectories.

● SYNTAX

FASTOPEN *drive*:=n *drive*:=n *drive*:=n *drive*:=n */switch*

FASTOPEN requires, at a minimum, one hard-disk drive letter, for the drive whose file and subdirectory name locations will be stored in RAM. You may specify from 1 to 4 drives on the FASTOPEN command line. FASTOPEN will not work with floppy disks.

If you do not explicitly indicate the maximum number of stored file and directory name locations, the default on each drive is 48. You can change the number of stored locations by following the drive letter with an equal sign (=) and a number from 10 to 999. However, if you are specifying more than one drive, the total of all stored locations cannot exceed 999.

● SWITCH

/X   Indicates that the file locations will be stored in expanded memory. You must have installed an expanded memory manager for this option to work.

● EXAMPLES

FASTOPEN C:

sets up RAM to store the locations of the last 48 opened files on drive C.

FASTOPEN C:=150 D:=100 /X

sets up RAM to store the locations of the last 150 opened files on drive C, and the last 100 on drive D. RAM will use expanded memory to store the file locations.

● **NOTES**   Each file name location will use 48 bytes of memory. If you indicate the maximum 999 files, you will use almost 48K of RAM. Each file extent entry will require another 16 bytes of RAM, or just under an additional 16K if you use the maximum of 999. In general, these high values, because of their costly RAM requirements, will reach a point of diminishing returns: they will not significantly enhance performance for the RAM they use, and may in some cases interfere with applications that have heavy RAM requirements of their own. Experiment to find the minimum numbers that will still enhance the performance of your system.

Do not use FASTOPEN with drives that have been reassigned using the SUBST command. Do not use FASTOPEN while Microsoft Windows is running, over a network, or from the DOS shell. Do not use third-party disk optimizers after loading FASTOPEN.

If you wish to change the FASTOPEN settings, you must reboot DOS first.

FC

Matches the contents of two files, or sets of files, and reports the differences between them.

● **SYNTAX**

   FC /switches drive:\path\file(s) drive\path\file(s)

FC requires the names of two files that you want to compare. You may include wildcard characters in the file names for comparison.

If you do so, DOS compares the files that match each other within the naming convention represented by the wildcard characters.

If either file set is not on the current drive or subdirectory, you must explicitly name the drive or subdirectory location of the files.

Files with extensions .BIN, .COM, .EXE, .LIB, .OBJ, or .SYS are compared as binary files unless you explicitly instruct DOS, by means of option switches, to do otherwise. All other files are compared as ASCII files unless you explicitly instruct DOS to do a binary comparison.

• SWITCHES

/A   Condenses the report of differences when comparing ASCII files. Instructs DOS to display only the beginning and end of differing lines.

/B   Instructs DOS to perform a binary comparison: DOS compares the files byte-by-byte and reports all differences between bytes at the same offset location in the two files. The /B switch cannot be used in combination with any other option switch, except the /nnnn switch.

/C   Instructs DOS to ignore case when comparing ASCII files. Characters in both files are treated as if they were uppercase.

/L   Forces an ASCII comparison of the files.

/LB n   Sets the maximum number of differing lines allowed in ASCII file comparisons. If differing lines exceed the number n, the comparison process ends. If this switch is not used, the default is 100 lines.

/N   Includes line numbers in an ASCII comparison report.

/T   Does not expand tabs to spaces in an ASCII comparison report. If this switch is not used, tabs are displayed as eight spaces.

/W   Condenses an ASCII comparison report by
           displaying all tabs and consecutive spaces as a
           single space. Tabs and spaces are only condensed
           in the display. This switch ignores spaces at the
           beginning and end of lines.

/nnnn   Indicates the number of lines (or bytes in binary
           format comparisons) that must match after a
           difference is recorded. If less than this number is
           found, the match is displayed in the report along
           with the differences. If this switch is not used, the
           default is 2.

• EXAMPLES

FC TEST.TXT TEST.BAK

performs an ASCII comparison between TEST.TXT and TEST.BAK.

FC /B TEST.TXT TEST.BAK

forces a binary comparison between TEST.TXT and TEST.BAK.

FC /C /L /N /W *.BIN *.BAK

forces an ASCII comparison between *.BIN and *.BAK, disregards
character case, displays line numbers in the report, and condenses
consecutive spaces.

• **NOTE**   FC can make comparisons of ASCII files on a line-by-
line basis and will compare files that are different sizes, ending the
comparison when it reaches the end of the shorter file. The output
report from FC can be quite long, and redirection to a disk file or the
printer is advisable. Refer to the sections titled *Piping* and *Redirecting
Output* in *Part One* for details.

FDISK

Can overwrite or erase data!

Partitions a hard disk for DOS.

● SYNTAX

FDISK /switch

Enter FDISK without parameters to start the FDISK program. FDISK is a menu-driven program that sets up partitions on your hard disk. Use FDISK to review current partition information, delete old partitions, and add new ones. A single partition may hold up to 2 gigabytes of data.

● SWITCH

/STATUS   Displays hard disk partition information without entering the program.

● EXAMPLE

FDISK /STATUS

displays your hard disk's partition information.

● NOTES
Before a hard disk can be formatted to accept data, It must be partitioned. In earlier versions of DOS, large hard disks required more than one partition because of early limits on hard disk size. Later versions of DOS corrected this. Most hard disks using DOS 6 need a single partition, unless they are installed on systems that share another operating system besides DOS.

FDISK is meant for system installers. It is normally not needed in the course of everyday use. Deleting a partition permanently deletes all the data stored on that partition.

FDISK only works on hard disks physically installed on your computer. FDISK does not work on a drive reassigned using the SUBST command. FDISK is not intended for network or INTERLNK drives.

See Also FORMAT

FIND

Locates and displays all occurrences of a specified character string in a specified file.

● SYNTAX

FIND */switches* "string" *drive:\path\file*

FIND requires that you include a character string on the command line. The character string must be enclosed in quotation marks. It is case-sensitive, meaning that uppercase letters will not match lowercase letters. If the string contains quotation marks, they should be enclosed in another set of quotation marks.

If you include a file specification, DOS reads the file and reports all occurrences of the character string in the file. Alternatively, you may supply redirected output via piping from another command instead of a file, and FIND will report occurrences of the string in the output. Refer to the sections titled *Piping* and *Redirecting Output* in *Part One* for details.

● SWITCHES

/C   Counts the number of lines in the file that contain a
      match for the character string, and reports the total
      only.

/I   Ignores letter case when searching for matching
      strings.

/N   Includes line numbers in the report of matching
      strings. If you include this option with the /C option,
      it is ignored.

/V   Reports only those lines that do not contain a match
      for the specified string. If you include this option with
      the /C option, DOS counts the number of lines that
      do not contain a match and reports that total.

● **NOTE**   You cannot use wildcard characters in filenames used
with FIND. However, you can nest a FIND command in a FOR command and execute FIND for each file in FOR's argument list. Refer
to *Appendix B* for more information regarding batch files.

● EXAMPLES

FIND "FIND" SAMPLE.TXT /C

reports the total number of lines in SAMPLE.TXT that contain the
string *FIND*.

FIND "Say""hello there"", DOS" SAMPLE.TXT

reports the lines in SAMPLE.TXT that contain the string *Say "hello
there", DOS*. Notice that each double-quote character contained
within the string is entered twice to include the additional quotation marks inside the test string.

CHKDSK /V | FIND "BAK" /N

uses the output of the CHKDSK /V command and displays all lines
that contain BAK. The display includes the relative line number of
each line.

FIND "" SAMPLE.TXT /C/V

reports the total number of lines in SAMPLE.TXT.

FORMAT

Can overwrite or erase data!

Prepares a blank disk for receiving and storing data, or creates a new blank disk from a used one.

● SYNTAX

FORMAT *target: /switches*

FORMAT requires that you specify a drive letter for the disk to format.

● USING FORMAT
When you run the FORMAT command to format your disks, FORMAT displays a message indicating the drive you are about to format, and prompts you to press Enter when ready to proceed. This gives you the opportunity to change the disk in the drive if necessary, or cancel the operation by pressing Ctrl-C.

When the formatting operation is complete, DOS displays a message showing the total number of bytes available on disk, how many bytes have been marked as "bad sectors" (that is, unusable because of some defect that DOS discovered), and how many bytes have been used by system files, if you indicated the /S option in the command line. DOS also indicates how data may be allocated on the newly formatted disks. DOS then asks if you would like to format another disk using the same parameters. If you enter **Y**, you are prompted to insert another disk, press Enter, and the formatting process repeats. Otherwise, you are returned to the DOS prompt.

If you supply the drive letter of a hard disk and your hard disk has a volume label, DOS prompts you to enter the volume label before it proceeds with the format.

● SWITCHES

/1   Formats a double-sided disk as a single-sided disk.

/4   Formats a single-density (160K) or double-density
            (360K) disk with the correct number of default
            tracks and sectors in a high-density (1.2Mb) drive.
            Be careful: some systems may not be able to read
            disks formatted with this switch.

/8   Formats 8 sectors per track on 5.25" floppy disks
            instead of the default, which is 9 for single- or
            double-density disks, or 15 for high-density disks.
            This option cannot be used with hard disks, nor
            can it be used with the /T or /V option.

/B   Formats a disk so as to leave room for the system
            files, although system files are not copied. Cannot
            be used with the /T or /S option. This switch is
            not needed in DOS 6; it is included only for com-
            patibility with earlier versions.

/F:*size*   Specifies the size, in kilobytes, of the disk to be
            formatted. Not to be used with /1, /8, /T, or /N
            options. The following parameters may be used
            for size:

            160K = 5.25" single-sided, 8 sectors/track
            180K = 5.25" single-sided, 9 sectors/track
            320K = 5.25" double-sided, 8 sectors/track
            360K = 5.25" double-sided, 9 sectors/track
            720K = 3.5" double-sided, 9 sectors/track
            1.2M = 5.25" high-density, 15 sectors/track
            1.44M = 3.5" high-density, 15 sectors/track
            2.88M = 3.5" extra-high-density, 30 sectors/track

/N:*nn*   Indicates the number of sectors per track, where
            nn is the number of sectors you specify. This
            option must be used together with the /T option.
            Do not use this parameter with the /8, /F, or /B
            options.

/Q   Specifies that formatting does not reinitialize
            tracks and sectors on a previously formatted disk.

/S   Transfers DOS system files to the formatted disk.
            Intended to make the disk "bootable"—that is,
            capable of loading DOS into memory when the
            computer is booted up while the disk is in the
            default boot drive (usually drive A).

/T:*nn*   Indicates the number of tracks on the disk, where
            nn is the number of tracks that you specify. This
            option must be used together with the /N option.
            Do not use this parameter with the /8, /F or /B
            options.

/U   Specifies unconditional reformatting. All data on a
            previously formatted disk is destroyed, and you
            will not be able to unformat this disk later.

/V   Prompts you to add a volume label to the disk
            after formatting. A volume label is a string, up to
            11 characters long, that can function as an
            identifying title for the disk. You cannot use the
            /V option with the /8 option.

/V:*label* Automatically adds a volume label to the disk
            after formatting, as indicated by :*label*.

● EXAMPLES

FORMAT A:

formats the disk in drive A, using current default parameters for
the drive type.

FORMAT A: /S /V

formats a disk in drive A, using current drive defaults, then copies
the system files to the disk, and prompts the user to enter a volume
label for that disk.

FORMAT A: /1 /8

formats a floppy disk in drive A as a single-sided disk with 8 sectors
per track. This format may be required by some early PC systems.

FORMAT A: /4
FORMAT A: /F:360K

formats a 5.25" double-density (360K) disk in a high-density (1.2Mb) drive.

```
FORMAT A: /T:80 /N:9
FORMAT A: /F:720K
```

formats a 3.5" low-density (720K) disk in a high-density (1.44Mb) drive.

• ERRORLEVEL CODES

0 = Format successful

3 = Format interrupted by Ctrl-C or Ctrl-Break

4 = Format interrupted by disk, data or other technical error

5 = User responded **N** to hard-disk safety prompt, "Proceed with format?"

• **NOTES**   Do not use the FORMAT command with drives that have been reassigned using the SUBST command, or over a network or INTERLNK drive. If you do not specify the data capacity of the floppy disk on the command line, DOS will format the floppy disk at the capacity of the disk drive. Always format disks at their correct data capacity (for example, 360K or 1.2Mb). Disks formatted at the incorrect capacity will perform extremely unreliably.

Always exercise extreme caution when using this command, to avoid accidentally formatting a disk that contains data you want to keep. A separate utility command, UNFORMAT, can help you recover from an accidental format in some cases. If the disk was previously formatted, it's usually not necessary to use the /U parameter or a switch that changes the size of the disk. This allows DOS to save the old file allocation table and root directory, and allow unformatting. Use the UNFORMAT command as soon as possible.

If the disk has never been formatted before, use the /U switch to save a little time.

Before you can use FORMAT on hard disks, an underlying, or *low-level*, format must be completed, and the hard disk must be partitioned using FDISK. The low-level format and partitioning is

ᶦusually completed by the manufacturer or dealer before you purchase the disk. If you find that you cannot successfully format your
hard disk, or that you cannot get your computer to acknowledge
the presence of a hard disk drive in your system, check with your
hard disk's documentation or ask your dealer if a low-level format
is required.

See Also   LABEL, UNFORMAT, VOLUME, FDISK

GRAPHICS

E

Allows graphics characters to be sent to an IBM-compatible
graphics printer using Shift-Prtsc.

● SYNTAX

GRAPHICS *printer drive:\path\file /switches*

Used without parameters, the GRAPHICS command will allow the
Shift-Prtsc key combination to send screen graphics characters to
an IBM graphics printer, or a printer that is fully compatible. In addition, to use this command, you must have a monitor that can display the IBM graphics character set.

You may specify the following alternate types of graphics printers
on the command line:

COLOR1 = IBM Color Printer with black ribbon

COLOR4 = IBM Color Printer with red, green, blue, black ribbon

COLOR8 = IBM Color Printer with cyan, magenta, yellow,
black ribbon

HPDEFAULT = Any Hewlett-Packard PCL printer

DESKJET = Hewlett-Packard DeskJet printer

GRAPHICS = IBM Personal Graphics printer, Proprinter, or Quietwriter

GRAPHICSWIDE = IBM Personal Graphics Printer with 11-inch carriage

LASERJET = Hewlett-Packard LaserJet printer

LASERJETII = Hewlett-Packard LaserJet II printer

PAINTJET = Hewlett-Packard PaintJet printer

QUIETJET = Hewlett-Packard QuietJet printer

QUIETJETPLUS = Hewlett-Packard QuietJet Plus printer

RUGGEDWRITER = Hewlett-Packard RuggedWriter printer

RUGGEDWRITERWIDE = A Hewlett-Packard RuggedWriter (wide) printer

THERMAL = IBM PC-convertible Thermal Printer

THINKJET = Hewlett-Packard ThinkJet printer

Use the *file* parameter (with *drive:\path* if required) to specify the name and location of a *printer profile file*, containing information about all supported printers. If you do not supply this parameter, DOS looks for a file named GRAPHICS.PRO in the current directory and in the same directory as GRAPHICS.COM.

• SWITCHES

/R — Reverses foreground and background. Normally, the screen shows light characters on a dark background. When printing, the light characters print as dark characters and the background is not printed. If you would like the printed output to resemble the appearance of the screen more closely, use this switch to print light characters on a dark background.

/B — Prints background color. This option is only available with the COLOR4 and COLOR8 printers. If you do not specify this switch, the background is not printed.

| /LCD | Prints characters from the IBM PC Convertible Liquid Crystal Display. |
| /PRINTBOX:*AAA* | Selects the size of the print box, where *AAA* is the printbox ID. tag, the first parameter following the printbox statement in your printer profile. Refer to your printer's configuration documentation for details regarding the Printbox Statement. If you are using DOS's GRAPHICS.PRO file for your printer information, *AAA* is either STD or LCD. |

● EXAMPLES

GRAPHICS

allows Shift-Prtsc to send IBM graphics characters to an IBM Graphics Printer.

GRAPHICS COLOR4 /B

prints on the red, green, blue, black IBM color printer, including background color.

GRAPHICS THERMAL /LCD

prints on the IBM Convertible thermal printer from the IBM convertible liquid crystal display.

● **NOTES**   GRAPHICS increases the size of DOS in RAM by about 700 bytes. GRAPHICS requires that your computer have a graphics adapter and monitor. Versions 4.0+ support EGA and VGA graphics modes.

If you have already loaded a printer profile and you want to load another one, the new profile must be smaller than the current one. Otherwise, you must restart your computer.

See Also   PRINT

HELP

Displays summaries of command syntax.

● SYNTAX

HELP *command*

Invoke the HELP command without parameters to begin DOS's interactive help system. DOS will list its standard line, batch, and CONFIG.SYS commands. To receive help with a particular command, move the cursor to the desired command and press Enter, or pick the command using the mouse, if you have one installed. Alternatively, you can get help for a particular command by invoking HELP followed by the command name.

Most commands include a syntax summary, notes, and examples. You can use the mouse or the keyboard to move between various menu options. If you are using the keyboard, you can select menu items by holding down the Alt key and pressing the keyboard key that corresponds to the highlighted character in the screen menu item.

HELP includes its own online help system. To access online help, select the Help keyword from the top line of the opening menu, or press F1 or Alt-H.

● EXAMPLES

HELP

starts DOS's interactive help system.

HELP DOSKEY

displays a short description of DOSKEY command syntax.

• **NOTE**   For a more condensed command summary, you may enter the command name, followed by /?, or DOSHELP, followed by the command name.

See Also   DOSHELP

INTERLNK

Redirects commands to Interlnk server drives or printer ports.

• SYNTAX

INTERLNK *client=server*

To use this command, you must first install the INTERLNK.EXE device driver in CONFIG.SYS. Refer to *Appendix A* for more information on CONFIG.SYS, and *Appendix C* for more information on INTERLNK.EXE.

Invoke INTERLNK without parameters to display the current status of the Interlink program.

The *client* parameter is a drive letter that indicates the client drive to be redirected. The *server* parameter specifies the drive letter of the Interlnk server that will be redirected. The server drive must be listed in the server column of the Interlnk server screen. Colons are not necessary when specifying drive letters with this command.

To cancel the redirection, leave out the *server* parameter.

• SWITCH

INTERLNK uses no optional command switches.

● EXAMPLES

INTERLNK F=C

redirects client drive F to server drive C. This command might be used to link a laptop computer to a desktop computer, to transfer files.

INTERLNK F=

cancels the redirection in the previous example.

See Also   INTERSRV

INTERSRV

Starts the Interlnk server, for transfer of files between Interlnk devices and drives.

● SYNTAX

INTERSRV *drive: /switches*

To use this command, you must first install the INTERLNK.EXE device driver in CONFIG.SYS. Refer to *Appendix A* for more information on CONFIG.SYS, and *Appendix C* for more information on INTERLNK.EXE.

The *drive:* parameter specifies a drive letter for the redirected drive. All drives are redirected by default.

● SWITCHES

/B
Forces black and white displays on color monitors and laptops that have trouble handling the default displays.

/BAUD:*rate*
Sets the maximum baud rate for data transfers. Valid rates are 9600, 19200, 38400, 57600, and 115200. Default is 115200.

/COM*n:address*
Specifies which serial port to use, where *n* is the number of the port. The optional *address* parameter specifies the port address. If you omit both parameters, the Interlnk server uses the first client serial port it finds. By default, all ports (parallel and serial) are scanned when you invoke INTERSRV.

/LPT*n:address*
Specifies which parallel port to use, where *n* is the number of the port. The optional *address* parameter specifies the port address. If you omit both parameters, the Interlnk server uses the first client parallel port it finds. By default, all ports (parallel and serial) are scanned when you invoke INTERSRV.

/V
Overrides timer conflicts, for use with computers whose internal timers cannot synchronize for jam serial communications.

/RCOPY
Downloads and installs Interlnk files from one computer to another. Computers must be connected with a 7-wire, null-modem serial cable. The MODE command must be available on the computer on which you are installing Interlnk.

/X=*drive:*
Specifies drive not to be redirected, where *drive:* is the drive letter.

• EXAMPLES

INTERSRV A: B: C:

starts the Interlnk server and redirects server drive A to client drive D, server drive B to client drive E, and server drive C to client drive F.

INTERSRV /X=A /COM2

specifies all server drives be redirected except drive A, and forces connection via COM2.

• NOTES   Interlnk does not redirect network drives, CD-ROM drives, or devices that already utilize a redirection interface. Do not use the following commands with the Interlnk server: CHKDSK, DEFRAG, DISKCOMP, DISKCOPY, FDISK, FORMAT, SYS, UN-DELETE, UNFORMAT.

Use either the /LPT or /COM switch when running the Interlnk server under Windows. Specify a switch other than the one your mouse is using to prevent a scan of your mouse port. For example, if your mouse is on COM1, use the /LPT switch.

Interlnk redirects drives in the order you specify. The first server drive is redirected to the first client drive, the second server drive to the second client drive, and so forth.

See Also   INTERLNK

KEYB

| E | | TSR |

Loads a nonstandard keyboard configuration into memory. The loaded configuration is taken from a library file, usually KEYBOARD.SYS.

● SYNTAX

KEYB *keyboard,codepage drive:\path\libraryfile /switches*

The *keyboard* parameter is a two-letter code indicating the nonstandard keyboard you want to load. If loading from KEYBOARD.SYS (the default keyboard library file), this code will represent a country, as shown in Table 4.1.

The *codepage* parameter is optional. It is a three-digit number representing a table that defines a foreign language character set to be used by the keyboard. If this parameter is not supplied, DOS uses the current code page. Refer to Table 4.1 for the correct code page number for supported countries.

The *libraryfile* parameter is used only if the library file is not KEYBOARD.SYS or if the location of the library file is not on the operating system's search path. See the PATH entry for more information regarding search paths.

Table 4.1: Keyboard Codes

Country	Code	Keyboard Code Page (Alternate)	Keyboard IDs
United States (default)	US	850 (437)	
Belgium	BE	850 (437)	
Brazil	BR	850 (437)	
Canadian (French)	CF	850 (863)	
Czechoslovakia (Czech)	CZ	852 (850)	
Czechoslovakia (Slovak)	SL	852 (850)	
Denmark	DK	850 (865)	
Finland	SU	850 (437)	
France	FR	850 (437)	120, 189

Table 4.1: Keyboard Codes (continued)

Country	Code	Keyboard Code Page (Alternate)	Keyboard IDs
Germany	GR	850 (437)	
Hungary	HU	852 (850)	
Italy	IT	850 (437)	141, 142
Latin America	LA	850 (437)	
Netherlands	NL	850 (437)	
Norway	NO	850 (865)	
Poland	PL	852 (850)	
Portugal	PO	850 (860)	
Spain	SP	850 (437)	
Sweden	SV	850 (437)	
Swiss (French)	SF	850 (437)	
Swiss (German)	SG	850 (437)	
United Kingdom	UK	850 (437)	166, 168
Yugoslavia	YU	852 (850)	

When invoked without parameters, KEYB displays the name of the currently logged nonstandard keyboard, its code page, and the code page for the console, if a nonstandard keyboard layout was previously installed.

● SWITCHES

/E   Specifies that an enhanced keyboard is installed on an Intel 8086-based (XT-type) computer.

/ID:*nnn*   Use the ID switch to designate the currently logged keyboard by means of its three-digit ID number (which is not the same as the code page), where *nnn* is the chosen ID number. This switch is used in addition to the standard two-letter keyboard code. It is required only for those countries that have more than one keyboard layout for the same character set.

● EXAMPLES

KEYB

displays the currently installed nonstandard keyboard configuration, if any.

KEYB UK

installs the United Kingdom keyboard.

KEYB UK,437 /ID:166

is an optional syntax that will install the United Kingdom keyboard.

● ERRORLEVEL CODES

0 = Installation was successful

1 = Invalid command line syntax

2 = Keyboard library file not found or invalid

3 = Could not load keyboard configuration

4 = Error with console device

5 = Requested code page was not prepared

6 = Code Page table not found

7 = Incorrect DOS version

• **NOTES**   Before you invoke KEYB, the code page you specify for *codepage* must be prepared for your system. Prepare the code page by first including the COUNTRY command in CONFIG.SYS, then invoking the NLSFUNC command.

Refer also to the commands NLSFUNC and MODE, and the COUNTRY command in *Appendix A*. Once you have prepared code page tables, you may use CHCP to switch between them.

Once a nonstandard keyboard is loaded, you can switch between the standard and nonstandard keyboard configurations. Press Ctrl-Alt-F1 to switch to the standard keyboard; press Ctrl-Alt-F2 to switch to the nonstandard configuration. If the configuration for the selected country supports typewriter mode, you can switch to that setting by pressing Ctrl-Alt-F7. DOS will not display any messages when you switch.

LABEL

Adds or modifies a disk volume label.

• **SYNTAX**

LABEL *target:label*

The LABEL command requires a drive letter on the command line. If you include the optional *label* parameter, DOS writes the specified volume label on the disk indicated by the drive letter. If you do not include the *label* parameter on the command line, DOS prompts you to enter the volume label. If you press Enter without entering a volume label, DOS assumes that you want to delete the current label, and prompts you to confirm the deletion. If you want to delete the current label, enter **Y**. Otherwise, enter **N**.

A disk volume label may be up to 11 characters long, and may include spaces. Do not use tabs or the following punctuation marks in a volume label:

    * ? & ^ / \ | , . ; : < > [ ] ( ) + = "

The space character and the following punctuation marks *are* valid:

    ! _ @ # $ % ~ ' − { }

● EXAMPLES

    LABEL C:

will cause DOS to prompt you to enter a volume label for a disk in drive C (often a hard disk).

    LABEL C:MY DATA

will write the volume label "MY DATA" on the disk in drive C.

● **NOTE**   Do not use LABEL on drives that have been reassigned using the SUBST command.

See Also   DIR, VOL

LH OR LOADHIGH

Loads terminate-and-stay-resident (TSR) software into reserved memory.

• SYNTAX

LH /switches drive:\path\ program

LOADHIGH /switches drive:\path\ program

TSR software is normally loaded into *conventional memory,* which is the area of RAM from 0 to 640K. The LH and LOADHIGH commands attempt to load the TSR program specified in the *program* parameter into *reserved memory,* the area of RAM between 640K and 1024K, provided that DOS can find available space. Otherwise, the program is loaded in conventional memory.

To use this command, you must first have loaded the HIMEM.SYS device driver plus an expanded memory manager that supports the Microsoft Extended Memory Specification for upper memory blocks (UMBs); for example, EMM386.EXE, which is supplied with MS-DOS. Use CONFIG.SYS to load these driver files. In addition, you must also include the UMB parameter in the DOS= command line in CONFIG.SYS. Refer to *Appendix A* for details on the DEVICE= and DOS= commands in CONFIG.SYS, and *Appendix C* for details regarding HIMEM.SYS and EMM386.EXE.

• SWITCHES

/L:*region1,minsize1;region2,minsize2 ...*

specifies regions of upper memory into which to load the program. If this switch is not used, DOS loads the program into the largest UMB it finds. Regions are numbered using integers beginning with 1. DOS loads the program into the largest UMB in the specified region, provided it can find a UMB that is larger than the program's load size.

You can specify more than one memory region in cases where a program uses more than one. Separate the region numbers on the command line with a semicolon.

Some programs expand in memory while running. If you are loading such a program, you can also indicate a minimum size for a UMB in the specified region (in bytes). DOS will load the program if it can find a UMB that is larger than the program's load size and the indicated minimum size. Separate the minimum size value from the region number using a comma.

/S

shrinks the UMB to its minimum size while loading. This switch helps maximize use of upper memory. You can use this switch only if you are also using the /L switch to specify a minimum size for UMBs.

• EXAMPLES

LH MOUSE

loads the mouse driver software into reserved memory.

LH /L:1,11504 SETVER.EXE

loads SETVER.EXE in memory region 1, provided there is a UMB of at least 11,504 bytes in that region.

• NOTES Not all TSR software can be loaded in reserved memory. To see if your software can utilize reserved memory, try the following: reboot, load the program with LOADHIGH, and invoke the MEM command. Note the amount of available conventional memory. Then reboot again, load the program normally, and invoke MEM. If MEM reports a greater amount of conventional RAM after loading with LOADHIGH than it does after loading the program normally, then LOADHIGH is loading the program in reserved memory.

The MEMMAKER command can help you analyze your system's use of memory and determine which drivers and programs can fit into UMBs. It can rewrite your AUTOEXEC.BAT file, adding LOADHIGH commands, with /L and /S switches as required. For more details, refer to the discussion of the *MEMMAKER* command in this chapter.

See Also MEM, MEMMAKER, DEVICEHIGH (*Appendix A*)

LOADFIX

Runs application software that may not load properly when DOS 6 occupies high memory.

● SYNTAX

LOADFIX *drive:\path* program

LOADFIX causes external applications to be loaded above the first 64K of conventional memory. Most applications have no need for LOADFIX.

If you try to run a program that ran under an earlier version of DOS and receive a "Packed file corrupt" message under DOS 6, try invoking the program with LOADFIX.

● EXAMPLE

LOADFIX FASTBACK

loads FASTBACK.EXE in conventional memory.

MD OR MKDIR

Creates a new subdirectory.

● SYNTAX

MD *drive:\path directory*
MKDIR *drive:\path directory*

MD requires that you provide a subdirectory name on the command line. If the subdirectory name is preceded by a backslash (\), it will be created one level below the root directory. If the name is preceded by a space, it will be created one level below the currently logged subdirectory.

If you include an existing subdirectory path, the new subdirectory will be created one level below the indicated path. If you include a drive letter, the subdirectory will be created on the existing drive.

● EXAMPLES

MD TEXT

creates a subdirectory named TEXT one level below the currently logged subdirectory.

MD \TEXT

creates a subdirectory named TEXT one level below the root directory.

MD \DATA\TEXT

creates a subdirectory named TEXT one level below the DATA subdirectory, if the DATA subdirectory already exists.

MD C:\DATA\TEXT

creates a subdirectory named TEXT one level below the DATA subdirectory on drive C, if C:\DATA already exists.

See Also   CD or CHDIR

Displays information on allocation of random access memory.

● SYNTAX

MEM */switches*

When invoked without option switches, MEM displays a summary of the amount and type of installed memory.

● SWITCHES

/Classify   Use this switch to list currently loaded programs, including the amount of memory each is using. /C also specifies this switch.

/Debug   Lists programs and system device drivers, including their RAM addresses. You cannot use the /Program switch with this switch. /D also specifies this command.

/Free   Lists the free areas of RAM, including address and size. If an expanded memory manager is installed and includes Upper Memory Blocks, this parameter also shows the largest UMB in each region of upper memory. You cannot use this switch with any other switch except /Page. /F also specifies this switch.

/Module   Displays RAM in use by a particular program.
program   You must specify a name of a loaded program after this switch. You cannot use this switch with any other switch except /Page. /M also specifies this switch.

/Page   Pauses after each screen of output. /P also specifies this switch.

● EXAMPLE

MEM /CLASSIFY

lists the amount and type of installed RAM, and how it is allocated among loaded programs.

• NOTE MEM finds extended memory above 1Mb if installed. MEM will only find expanded memory that conforms to the LIM 4.0 expanded memory specification. Refer to your expanded memory driver documentation for details.

MEMMAKER

Automatically configures your system's device drivers to optimize random-access memory (RAM).

• SYNTAX

MEMMAKER */switches*

MEMMAKER analyzes your current system configuration and rewrites CONFIG.SYS and AUTOEXEC.BAT (plus Windows' SYSTEM.INI if necessary) to make optimal use of your system's random-access memory (RAM). If you invoke MEMMAKER without command-line switches, the program presents you with a full screen, menu- driven RAM optimization system.

For more detailed information on MEMMAKER, refer to *Part Two*.

As MEMMAKER processes, it presents you with a series of choices. First you can choose between Custom or Express setup. Express setup uses default responses to most configurable options and is faster. Custom setup is for experienced users, allowing you to fine-tune memory requirements to your liking. Custom setup takes more time and requires that you be familiar with upper memory, device drivers, and the memory-resident programs on your system.

Remaining choices depend on the particulars of your system. You can accept the default response by pressing Enter or cycle through the available options by pressing the spacebar until your desired option appears on the screen. Then, press Enter to accept the displayed option.

MEMMAKER includes an extensive online help system. To access online help, press F1.

MEMMAKER will restart your computer twice during processing. If it appears to stop for several minutes, restart your computer by turning it off and back on again. MEMMAKER includes internal system recovery routines if you have to do this.

• SWITCHES

/BATCH   Runs unattended (batch) mode. Mem-Maker assumes default responses for all prompts.

/SWAP:*drive*   Specifies your current startup drive, where *drive* is the drive letter. Use this switch if your startup disk drive changed after your computer started. Do not use this switch with Microsoft DoubleSpace or Stacker 2.0 compressed drives.

/UNDO   Undo the most recent changes made by MEMMAKER. Restart MEMMAKER using this switch if your system doesn't work properly after MEMMAKER completes or if you are not satisfied with your new memory configuration.

/W:*size1,size2* Specifies the amount of upper-memory space for Windows translation buffers; Windows requires two regions in upper memory for these buffers, where *size1* is the first region, *size2* is the second, in kilobytes (K). Default is two 12K regions of upper memory (/W:12,12). If you don't use Windows, you can specify /W:0,0 and save some upper memory for other programs.

● EXAMPLES

MEMMAKER /BATCH

starts MEMMAKER in batch mode, and automatically rewrites system configuration files using all default responses for your system.

MEMMAKER /UNDO

starts MEMMAKER and reverses the changes made using the previous example.

● ERRORLEVEL CODES

● **NOTES** After MemMaker completes, you can review status messages by viewing the contents of the MEMMAKER.STS file, which will reside in the same directory as MEMMAKER.EXE.

MEMMAKER stores the original version of AUTOEXEC.BAT as AUTOEXEC.UMB, CONFIG.SYS as CONFIG.UMB, and Windows' SYSTEM.INI as SYSTEM.UMB. You can undo MEMMAKER's changes by deleting the revised versions and renaming the files with .UMB extensions. However, if you undo the revisions on any one file, undo the revisions on all the others as well.

See Also CONFIG.SYS and DEVICEHIGH (*Appendix A*), EMM386 (*Appendix C*), LH, MEM

MODE

| E | | TSR |

Performs various functions relating to the transfer of data between the processor, screen, printer and keyboard. Specifically, the MODE command

- Sets the parallel printer mode
- Sets serial communication protocols
- Redirects parallel printer output
- Sets the video mode
- Shifts screen left or right
- Sets screen length and width
- Prepares and selects code pages
- Sets key repetition rates
- Displays the status of attached devices

● SYNTAX

To set the parallel printer mode:

MODE lpt*n*: cols=*c* lines=*l* retry=*r*

Alternate syntax:

MODE lpt*n*: *c,l,r*

You must specify a parallel printer device name as LPT followed by a number from 1 to 3, depending on the number of parallel ports on your system. *C* indicates the number of columns (always equal to the number of text characters) per line. *L* indicates the number of printed lines per inch. *R* indicates how DOS should react if the printer is not accepting data, where *r* is replaced with one of four possible parameters:

B   Return "busy" code if printer is not accepting data.

E   Return a DOS error message indicating that the printer is not accepting data.

N   Abort data transmission to the printer port with the "Abort, Retry, Ignore, Fail?" error message. This indicates that DOS should not retry sending data.

P   Retry sending data until printer accepts it. To break out of this loop, press Ctrl-Break.

R   Resets the port to "Ready" status; sends the data (same as P parameter in DOS versions 3 and earlier).

Do not use any of these *r* values if you are sending data over a network.

To set serial communication protocols:

MODE com*n*: baud=*bb* parity=*p* data=*d* stop=*s* retry=*r*

Alternate syntax:

MODE com*n*: *bb,p,d,s,r*

Before you initialize serial communication settings, refer to your documentation for the peripheral device to determine the correct setting for these parameters.

The first parameter indicates the communication port that you want to use, where *n* after COM is the number of the port. Baud=*bb* indicates the baud rate. Only the first two digits of the baud rate are significant; for example, baud=9600 can also be expressed as baud=96.

Parity=*p* indicates the parity type, where *p* can be one of the following values:

N   No parity

E   Even parity

O   Odd parity

M   Stick Odd parity

S   Stick Even parity

Default is Even parity.

Data=*d* indicates the number of databits, where *d* is a value from 5 through 8 (the default is 7). Stop=*s* indicates the number of stopbits, where *s* is either 1, 1.5, or 2. (The default is 2 if the baud rate is 110; otherwise, it is 1.)

Retry=*r* is used if the peripheral device is a printer. It indicates how DOS should react if the printer is not accepting data, where *r* is replaced with one of four possible parameters, the same as those used with the retry=*r* argument when setting parallel communication protocols.

If you are using the alternate syntax, MODE requires that the parameters be in their specific position as shown in the alternate syntax line. If you do not specify a value for any parameter, you must still include the comma before the next parameter.

To redirect parallel printer output to a serial port:

MODE lpt*n*:=com*n*:

You must specify a valid parallel and serial port number for your system, where *n* is the port number. Before directing parallel output to a serial port, use the MODE command to initialize the serial communications parameters, as explained earlier.

To set the video mode:

MODE *videomode* ,*length* ,*shift* ,T

The *video mode* parameter may be one of several possible values. Following are the *videomode* codes supported by MODE:

40 or 80	Indicates the number of characters per line.
BW40 or BW80	Specifies black-and-white on a CGA display, plus the number of characters per line.
CO40 or CO80	Specifies a color monitor and specifies the number of characters per line.

MONO   Specifies monochrome display (80
                        characters per line).

The optional *length* parameter indicates the number of lines that
your monitor can display. It may be supplied only if the ANSI.SYS
device driver was loaded in the CONFIG.SYS file. See *Appendix B*
and *Appendix C* for details. The screen length may be any number of
lines that your monitor is capable of displaying; refer to your
monitor and graphics card documentation for details.

The optional *shift* parameter shifts the screen display one or two
characters to the right or left. Replace *shift* with *R* to shift right or *L*
to shift left. This parameter cannot be used on the same command
line with the *length* parameter; use one or the other, not both. If you
use the *shift* parameter, you may also supply the optional *T*
parameter. If this parameter is supplied, MODE will display a test
pattern on the screen, allowing you to visualize the results of the
shifting.

To set screen length and width:

MODE CON LINES=*nn* COLS=*nn*

This command will work only if the ANSI.SYS device driver was
loaded in the CONFIG.SYS file. You must use CON as the first
parameter to indicate that you are setting lines and columns for the
console device. The *nn* in Lines=*nn* indicates the number of screen
lines to display. (Be certain that your monitor is capable of displaying the number of lines you specify.) The *nn* in COLS=*nn* indicates
the number of screen columns, or number of characters per line, to
display.

To prepare code pages (foreign character sets) for use by a
peripheral device:

MODE device **CODEPAGE PREPARE=((**code page list**)**
drive:\path\file **)**

The *device* parameter indicates one of the standard DOS output
devices (CON, PRN, or LPT1–3). Serial communications ports are
not a valid device in this context.

A *code page* is a three-digit number referencing a particular foreign character set used by the printer, screen, or keyboard. Following are the code pages and countries supported by MODE:

437   United States

850   Multilingual (Latin I)

852   Slavic (Latin II)

860   Portuguese

863   Canadian-French

865   Nordic

Refer to the CHCP, KEYB, and NLSFUNC commands, as well as the COUNTRY command in *Appendix A*, for more details on foreign fonts and how they are used. The *code page list* parameter consists of any number of valid code pages, separated by commas.

Following the code page list, include the name of the code page information file. This file has a .CPI extension, and contains the device definitions attached to the foreign fonts you have specified. The CPI extension is not required, but you must include a drive letter and subdirectory path if the code page information file is not located on the currently logged drive and path.

To make a particular code page active:

MODE *device* **CODEPAGE SELECT=**nnn

The *device* parameter indicates one of the standard DOS output devices (CON, PRN, LPT1–3) for which a code page has been previously prepared, where *nnn* indicates the number of the prepared code page to make active. You may substitute *CP* for CODEPAGE and *SEL* for SELECT in the above syntax. You must use the DEVICE command in CONFIG.SYS to install the DISPLAY.SYS driver file to use MODE for code-page switching.

To reinstate a code page that has been lost:

MODE *device* **CODEPAGE REFRESH**

To see a display of the current code page setup:

MODE *device* **CODEPAGE /STATUS**

The *device* parameter indicates one of the standard DOS output devices (CON, PRN, LPT1–3) for which a code page has been prepared.

To set key repetition rates:

MODE CON RATE=nn **DELAY=**n

where nn indicates the approximate number of times per second (1 to 32) a key will repeat when it is held down. The number supplied in place of nn does not correspond to the actual number of times per second the key repeats; lower numbers repeat slightly faster than their value, higher numbers repeat slightly slower.

DELAY=n indicates the amount of time required to hold a key down before it begins repeating, where n is a delay value. If you set the rate, you must also include a setting for the delay. The range of valid delay values is from 1 to 4, where 1 equals ¼ second, 2 equals ½ second, 3 equals ¾ second, and 4 equals 1 second.

To display the status of a particular device on all versions:

MODE *device* **/STATUS**

The *device* parameter indicates the device whose status you want to check. Valid device names are CON, PRN, LPT1–3, and COM1–4. The /STATUS parameter is used only when the output of the device you are checking was previously redirected to another device.

● EXAMPLES

MODE COM1 BAUD=9600 PARITY=NONE DATA=8 STOP=1
RETRY=B

sets the communication protocol on the first serial port to 9600 baud, no parity, eight databits, and one stop bit, for a printing device.

MODE LPT1=COM1

redirects standard parallel printer output to the first serial port.

MODE LPT1 /STATUS

checks the status of a redirected parallel printer. Without the /STATUS switch, MODE would remove redirection from the parallel port.

MODE CON CODEPAGE PREP=((865,437) C:\DOS\EGA)

prepares the code pages for Denmark and Germany for use by an EGA-type display device. (This example assumes that the code page file is named EGA.CPI, located on the C:\DOS subdirectory.)

MODE CON RATE=25 DELAY=1

sets keyboard repetition rates to 16 per second after holding the key down for ¼ second.

MODE CON

displays the status of all devices on the system.

MORE

Forces DOS to display output one screen at a time instead of continuous scrolling.

● SYNTAX

MORE < *drive:\path*file(s)

Alternate syntax:

command [parameter(s)] I **MORE**

There are two ways to use the MORE command:

• If you would like to display the contents of a data file on the screen, enter MORE followed by the redirection symbol for input (<), then by the name of the file. Wildcard characters are not allowed.

- If you would like to display the output of another command, enter the command and any required parameters followed by the redirection symbol for piping (|), then by MORE.

When you use MORE to display output, the display will stop each time the screen fills with information. To continue the display, press any key.

● EXAMPLES

MORE < REPORT.TXT

displays the contents of REPORT.TXT on the screen, pausing each time the screen is full.

TYPE REPORT.TXT | MORE

has the same result as the previous example. In this case, the output of the TYPE command is redirected to MORE.

See Also   TYPE

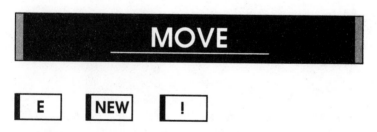

MOVE

| E | | NEW | | ! |

Can overwrite or erase data!

Moves files to different locations. Can rename subdirectories.

● SYNTAX

MOVE *source:\path*\file(s) *target:\path\file(s)*

MOVE requires that you specify the name of a source file or files. You can include a drive letter or directory path if the source file is not on the currently-logged directory. Wildcards are allowed, and will move groups of files that match the wildcard specification.

MOVE has the same effect as copying a file to a new location and then deleting the file in the original location, in a single command. You can rename a file as you move it by specifying a new name for the file. You can specify only one file as the source if you are renaming it at the same time. If you do not specify a *target* location, DOS attempts to move the source file to the currently logged directory.

Any file in the target location that has the same name as a source file is automatically overwritten.

You can rename a directory using the MOVE command by specifying the old directory name as the source and a new directory name as the target.

● SWITCH

MOVE has no option switches.

● EXAMPLE

MOVE C:\TEMP C:\NEWLOCA

If C:\TEMP is a file, it is moved from the root directory to the C:\NEWLOCA directory. If C:\TEMP is a directory, it is renamed C:\NEWLOCA.

● NOTES
You cannot move a directory to a new location in the directory tree. For example, if C:\TEMP and C:\NEWLOCA were both directories, the following command would not work:

MOVE C:\TEMP C:\NEWLOCA\TEMP

However, in the above example, if C:\TEMP were a *file*, it would be moved to the C:\NEWLOCA directory.

See Also   COPY, XCOPY, DEL

MSAV

Scans memory and hard disks for the presence of computer viruses.

● SYNTAX

MSAV *drive:\path /switches*

If you invoke the MSAV command without parameters, you are presented with a full screen, menu-driven system. You may select the drive or directory whose files you want to analyze and specify various options. You can use a mouse or the keyboard to move between various menu options. If you are using the keyboard, you can move between menu items using the arrow keys and select items by pressing the spacebar. Alternatively, you can select items by holding down the Alt key and pressing the keyboard key that corresponds to the highlighted character in the screen menu item.

MSAV includes an extensive online help system. To access online help, press F1.

Alternatively, you can select the drive, directory and options by entering the drive letter on the command line when you invoke MSAV, along with various control switches.

● SWITCHES

/S   Scans files on the specified drives and directories but does not remove viruses. This switch is default.

/C   Scans files on the specified drives and directories and removes viruses.

/R	Creates a report on disk (MSAV.RPT) that lists the number of files checked, the number of viruses found, and the number of viruses removed.
/A	Excludes drives A and B.
/L	Excludes network drives.
/N	Turns off display while scanning and displays MSAV.RPT file when complete.
/P	Run MSAV in graphics mode.
/F	Turns off the display of filenames. Use with the /N or /P switch.
/videomode	Forces a specific display mode, where videomode is the display you specify. Valid modes are:

    25 = 25 line display (default)
    28 = 28 line display (EGA and VGA only)
    43 = 43 line display (EGA and VGA only)
    50 = 50 line display (VGA only)
    60 = 60 line display (Video 7 only)
    IN = Forces color display
    BW = Forces black and white display
    MONO = Forces monochrome display
    LCD = forces LCD display
    FF = Fast screen updates on CGA displays
    BF = Forces BIOS display
    NF = Disables alternate fonts
    BT = Allows graphics mouse in Windows

/NGM	Forces default mouse character.
/LE	Reverses left/right mouse buttons.
/IM	Disables mouse.
/PS2	Resets mouse cursor.

● EXAMPLE

MSAV /A/P

runs MSAV, excluding floppy drives A and B and forcing graphics mode.

MSBACKUP

Can overwrite or erase data!

Backs up and restores files.

● SYNTAX

MSBACKUP *specfile /switches*

● SWITCHES

/TF   (Type=Full) Backs up all files named in the specification file.

/TI   (Type=Incremental) Backs up all files named in the specification file that have changed since the last backup.

/TD   (Type=Differential) Backs up all files named in the specification file that have changed since the last full backup.

/BW   Starts MSBACKUP in black-and-white for monitors that have trouble displaying the screen colors.

/LCD   Starts MSBACKUP in laptop video mode.

/MDA   Starts MSBACKUP in monochrome video mode.

● EXAMPLE

MSBACKUP MY-FILES

starts the backup program using (or creating) a specification file called MY-FILES.SET.

● ERRORLEVEL CODES

0 = Normal Completion

1 = No files were found to back up

2 = Some files were not backed up because of errors

3 = BACKUP interrupted by operator's CTRL-C

4 = Premature termination because of errors

● **NOTE**   The first time you run MSBACKUP, it analyzes your system to configure itself for the type of monitor and floppy disks you are using. If you change your system, use the **CONFIGURE** command on the opening menu to change MSBACKUP's configuration and test the new setup. If the files you intend to back up will not fit onto a single floppy disk, MSBACKUP will prompt you to insert another. You must have sufficient disks handy to hold all the files you are backing up. One 5.25" high-density disk stores about 1.2Mb of data. A 5.25" double-sided disk stores a little less than one-third as much. A 3.5" high-density disk stores 1.44Mb; a 3.5" low-density disk stores half as much.

MSD

Produces a technical diagnostic and information report for your system.

• SYNTAX

MSD /switches

MSD may be invoked without switches, in which case it will display an interactive, menu-driven display of technical information about your computer. To see information on any particular device, press the highlighted letter in the device's menu box. To access MSD's pop-down menus, press Alt-F (for files), or Alt-U (for Utilities). To exit MSD, press Alt-FX, or press the F3 function key.

Alternatively, you can invoke MSD with switches that control MSD's output.

• SWITCHES

/B	Forces Black and white mode on color displays that do not correctly display MSD output.
/I	Bypass initial hardware detection. Use this switch if MSD does not run properly.
/Fdrive:\path\filename	Runs full reporting. Prompts for name and company information, then writes a report on disk using the drive: \path and filename parameters you specify.
/Pdrive:\path\filename	Runs partial reporting. (Bypasses prompts for name and company information.) Writes a report on disk using the drive: \path and filename parameters you specify.
/Sdrive:\path\filename	Writes a short summary report on disk using the drive: \path and filename parameters you specify.

If you do not specify a drive: \path or filename, MSD displays the report on the screen.

• EXAMPLE

MSD /PC:\DOS\MSDRPT.TXT

runs MSD and writes a report to the file C:\DOS\MSDRPT.TXT.

• NOTES   MSD reports on the following aspects of your system:

Computer	Manufacturer, processor type, and bus type; ROM BIOS manufacturer, version and date; keyboard type; DMA controller configuration; math coprocessor status.
Memory	Map of the Upper Memory Area (640K to 1024K).
Video	Video card manufacturer, model, and type; video BIOS version and date; current video mode.
Network	If found, any network-specific configuration information.
Operating System	Version, location in memory, startup drive, current environment settings, and directory from which MSD was run.
Mouse	Driver version, mouse type, mouse interrupt, request line (IRQ) number, and other configuration information.
Other Adapters	Game card status for one or two game devices or joysticks.
Disk Drives	Size and number of bytes free on local and remote drives.
LPT Ports	Port addresses and status of each.
COM Ports	Port addresses, current communications parameters, and status of each.
IRQ Status	Configuration of the hardware IRQs.
TSR Programs	(Terminate-and-Stay-Resident Programs) Name, location in memory, and size of each.
Device Drivers	Names of all drivers installed when MSD is run.

See Also MEM

NLSFUNC

Loads national language support functions, allowing you to switch international character set tables in RAM.

• SYNTAX

NLSFUNC *drive:\path\countryfile*

If you want to use the CHCP command to switch code pages for multiple foreign language character sets, invoke this command first. You need only invoke the command once per session; if you switch character sets often, place this command in the AUTOEXEC.BAT file.

The NLSFUNC command may be invoked without parameters. If you do so, DOS uses the country-specific information found in the COUNTRY.SYS file to support code page switching between international character sets using the CHCP command.

If you are using a file other than COUNTRY.SYS, or if COUNTRY.SYS cannot be found along the DOS search path, specify the correct file name and search path on the command line when you invoke NLSFUNC.

• EXAMPLE

NLSFUNC C:\SYS\COUNTRY.SYS

loads national language support functions from COUNTRY.SYS, located in the C:\SYS subdirectory.

● **NOTE**   The default value for the country information file is defined by the COUNTRY command in CONFIG.SYS. If this command is not present in CONFIG.SYS, NLSFUNC looks for a file named COUNTRY.SYS in the root directory of the startup drive (usually C). If NLSFUNC cannot locate COUNTRY.SYS, it will not return an error message, but the CHCP command will return an error message, "Cannot open specified country information file."

See Also   CHCP

PATH

Specifies a list of subdirectories (the *search path*) where DOS is to look for executable program files.

● **SYNTAX**

   PATH *drive:\path ; drive:\path ...*

If invoked without parameters, PATH displays the current search path, if any.

If you want to create or change the search path, invoke PATH followed by a list of the drives and subdirectories where you want DOS to look for program files. Drive letters must be followed by colons. Subdirectory names must be preceded by a backslash (\).

If you do not include a drive letter, DOS will assume that the subdirectory is on the currently logged drive. Otherwise, it always looks for the subdirectory on the specified drive.

The various locations included in the search path must be separated from the others by a semicolon (;). To delete the entire path, use a semicolon as this command's only parameter.

The entire PATH command can include up to 127 characters.

● EXAMPLES

    PATH

displays the search path or the message "No path" if not found.

    PATH ;

clears all search-path settings and instructs DOS to search only the current directory.

    PATH C:\DOS;C:\WORD;C:\LOTUS;C:\SYS;C:\

instructs DOS to look for program files on drive C:, on subdirectories \DOS, \WORD, \LOTUS, \SYS, and the root directory.

    PATH \DOS;\WORD;\LOTUS;\SYS;\

instructs DOS to look for program files on the same set of subdirectories as the previous example; however, DOS will look for them on whatever drive is currently logged.

● NOTE   The PATH command creates a search path for program files only. Program files have the extensions .EXE, .COM, or .SYS. To create a search path for data files, use the APPEND command.

See Also   APPEND

POWER

Reduces power usage when your system is idle. Intended for users of battery-operated laptop and portable systems.

● SYNTAX

POWER *ADV:status|STD|OFF /switch*

You can invoke POWER without optional parameters to display the current power-conservation setting.

To set up power conservation, invoke power with the ADV:*status* parameter, where *status* is one of the following codes:

MAX   Maximum power conservation.

REG   Balance power conservation with device performance (default).

MIN   Minimum power conservation. Use when devices perform poorly under one of the other settings.

POWER may also be invoked with one of the following parameters:

OFF   Turns off power conservation.

STD   Uses your computer's internal power-conservation device, if it conforms to the Advanced Power Management (APM) specification. Consult your computer's documentation for details. If your computer does not support the APM specification, STD turns off power conservation.

● SWITCH

/LOW   Forces POWER to be loaded in conventional memory. By default, POWER loads into the upper memory area, if available.

● EXAMPLE

POWER ADV:MAX

enables maximum power conservation.

● **NOTE**   Use the DEVICE command in CONFIG.SYS to install POWER.EXE before using the POWER command. For details about

DEVICE and CONFIG.SYS, refer to *Appendix A*. For details about POWER.EXE, refer to *Appendix C*.

Sets aside a portion of RAM to be used for printing a series of files in the background while you continue to work with DOS.

● SYNTAX

PRINT */switches drive:\path\file(s) /switches*

If invoked without parameters, PRINT displays the status of the print *queue* (the list of files to be printed).

To configure DOS for background printing, enter the PRINT command followed by whatever options you desire (or none if the default values are acceptable) and a file name. Wildcard characters are permitted in file names. Each time you invoke PRINT with file names, the files are added to the print queue, up to the maximum specified by the /Q switch (see the Switches section). Maximum length for a filename (including its path) is 64 characters. DOS sends the contents of the file to a buffer in RAM, which in turn sends the data to the printing device, while allowing you to continue to invoke other operating system commands or application software.

Each file name, including its subdirectory location, may be up to 64 characters long.

● SWITCHES

When background printing is active, DOS is alternating very quickly between the foreground processing and the background printing. Optional parameters allow you to control which output device receives the output, how memory is split between printing and processing, how to allocate the time spent on each, and the maximum number of files that may be lined up for printing.

The /D switch, if used, must be first on the command line after the PRINT command.

The /D, /B, /U, /M, /S, and /Q switches configure the background printing environment; therefore, they may be used only once per session, the first time you invoke PRINT. The /C and /P switches must be preceded by a file name. All switches may be followed by file names, except the /Q switch, which may not be used on the same command line with a file name.

The least confusing way to use the PRINT command is to invoke it once with the configuration switches, then a second time to add file names to the queue.

/B:*buffer size*	Specifies the size, in bytes, of the printer buffer. Default is 512 bytes. The maximum size is 16,384 bytes. A larger buffer speeds printing, but requires additional RAM that may be needed by other commands.
/D:*device*	Specifies the output device name. If you do not use this switch on the command line (it must be the first switch following PRINT), DOS will prompt you to enter the device name. Default is PRN, the first parallel port on your system. Other possible output device names are LPT1 through LPT3 or COM1 though COM4. Do not use a colon following the device name.
/M:*ticks*	Specifies the maximum number of internal clock ticks DOS will take to send a character to the printer. Default is 2. The maximum value is 255.
/Q:*queue size*	Specifies the maximum number of files allowed in the print queue. The minimum number of files is 4, the maximum is 32. Default is 10.

/S:*slice*	Specifies the maximum number of internal clock ticks DOS will allow for foreground processing. Default is 8. The maximum value is 255.
/T	Removes all files from the print queue.
/U:*ticks*	Specifies the number of ticks on the computer's internal clock that DOS will wait before giving up and returning to foreground processing if the printer is not ready to receive data. Default is 1.
file name /C	Removes the indicated file name from the print queue. If additional file names follow this switch, they are removed as well.
file name /P	Adds the indicated file name to the print queue. If additional file names follow this switch, they are added to the queue also.

● EXAMPLES

PRINT /D:COM1 /Q:32 /B:4096 /S:20 /M:4 /U:2

directs the printing output to the first serial port, allows 32 file names in the print queue, sets a buffer size of 4K, sets the foreground processing time to 20 clock ticks, sets the background printing time to 4 clock ticks, and waits for 2 ticks if the printer is busy.

PRINT C:\REPORT*.TXT

prints all files in the C:\REPORT subdirectory with the .TXT extension.

PRINT C:\REPORT\REPORT3.TXT /C
C:\REPORT\REPORT3.BAK /P

removes C:\REPORT\REPORT3.TXT from the print queue and adds C:\REPORT\REPORT3.BAK to the print queue.

● NOTE The PRINT utility only works from DOS. It has no effect on printing commands that are invoked from within other applications. It can print text files while other applications are running; depending on the specific application and the switch settings for PRINT, it may cause a noticeable reduction in processing speed.

Disk accessing interrupts background printing. Programs that access the disk frequently will degrade the performance of PRINT.

PROMPT

Changes the appearance of the DOS system prompt. Sends Escape codes to ANSI.SYS.

● SYNTAX

PROMPT *prompt string*

Using PROMPT without parameters will cause DOS to display its default system prompt, which is the letter of the currently logged drive followed by a greater-than symbol; for example, C>.

You may specify a custom prompt string, consisting of any character string you wish, and DOS will display the string as the system prompt.

Certain special effects characters may be added to the prompt string:

$_	Moves to next line
$$	Dollar sign ($)
$b	Piping symbol (	)
$d	Current date
$e	ESC character
$g	Greater-than symbol (>)
$h	Backspace
$l	Less-than symbol (<)

$n   Current drive

$p   Currently logged drive and directory

$q   Equal sign (=)

$t   Current time

$v   DOS version number

If you have loaded the ANSI.SYS driver file in CONFIG.SYS, you may use the $e character to send Escape sequences for keyboard and cursor control to ANSI.SYS. See *Appendix A* and *Appendix C* for more details.

● EXAMPLES

PROMPT pg

sets the system prompt to include the currently logged subdirectory, followed by a greater-than symbol; for example: C:\DOS>.

PROMPT Please enter DOS command:$_$p$g

sets the system prompt to ask for command entry, and places the current path on the next line.

When the ANSI.SYS driver is loaded on a system with a color monitor

PROMPT $E[0;36;1;44m PROMPT $E[2J PROMPT pg

sets the screen to bright cyan text on a blue background, clears the screen, and displays the currently logged subdirectory in the DOS prompt. Refer to *Appendix C* for more details on using ANSI.SYS Escape codes in DOS commands.

● NOTES   The special effects characters in the prompt string are not case-sensitive; that is, they work in either upper- or lowercase. ANSI.SYS is case sensitive, however; be careful when sending Escape codes to ANSI.SYS.

You can define a special command prompt to use if you switch to DOS from within Windows 3.1. Use the SET command to create a value for an environmental variable named WINPMT. This variable accepts any value that PROMPT accepts and will display that value as the prompt when you switch to DOS from within Windows.

RD OR RMDIR

Removes empty subdirectories.

● SYNTAX

RD *drive:\path\subdirectory*
RMDIR *drive:\path\subdirectory*

RD requires that you supply the name of a completely empty subdirectory, that is, a subdirectory that does not contain any files. You cannot remove the currently logged subdirectory. If the subdirectory that you want to remove is located on a different drive or nested below other subdirectories, you must include the full subdirectory path to the unwanted directory on the command line.

● EXAMPLES

RD OLDDIR

removes an empty subdirectory named OLDDIR located on a level just below the current subdirectory.

RD \OLDDIR

removes an empty subdirectory named OLDDIR located one level below the root directory on the currently logged drive.

RD C:\WORD\OLDDIR

removes an empty subdirectory named OLDDIR one level below the WORD subdirectory, which is just below the root directory on drive C.

● **NOTES** Directories that contain hidden or system files may appear empty, but cannot be removed until the hidden files are deleted or moved from the directory. To view hidden or system files, refer to the DIR command (/A:H or /A:S switch). To change the attributes of hidden or system files, refer to the ATTRIB command.

Some application software packages create hidden files. Some may have their attributes changed and may then be erased without problems; others are created as part of copy-protection schemes devised by software developers. Be very careful when manipulating hidden files; if you delete them, you may render your application software unusable. If you are in doubt regarding the purpose of any hidden files in your subdirectories, contact technical support for the software packages you are using.

You cannot remove your root directory, the currently-logged directory, or a directory that has been reassigned using the SUBST command.

See Also   ATTRIB, CD, CHDIR, DIR, MD, MKDIR

REN OR RENAME

Changes file names.

● **SYNTAX**

REN *drive:\path\oldfile drive:\path\newfile*
RENAME *drive:\path\oldfile drive:\path\newfile*

The REN command requires an old file name and a new file name. When invoked, the command changes the old name to the new. Wildcard characters may be used to rename groups of files, but the wildcard specification must match between the old name and new.

If the old file is not located in the current drive or subdirectory, you may specify the drive and path name as part of the old file name parameter. It is not necessary to repeat the drive and path names with the new file name; DOS will keep the renamed file in its original location.

● **NOTE**   You cannot use the RENAME command to rename subdirectories, or to rename the path location of files. To rename a subdirectory, refer to the MOVE command.

● EXAMPLES

    REN REPORT.TXT SALES.RPT

changes the name of REPORT.TXT to SALES.RPT.

    REN C:\WORD*.BAK *.OLD

changes the names of all files with the extension .BAK on the C:\WORD subdirectory so that they now have the extension .OLD.

See Also   COPY, XCOPY

REPLACE

Can overwrite or erase data!

Selectively updates files on a target directory by replacing them with files of the same name on a source directory, or adds files to the target directory from the source.

• SYNTAX

REPLACE *source:\path\file(s) target:\path /switches*

REPLACE requires two parameters: source file names (wildcard characters are allowed) and a target drive, where the replacement files are to be copied. Source file names may include a drive letter and subdirectory path, and the target drive may include a subdirectory path as well. The target parameter does not include file names or wildcard characters.

REPLACE differs from the COPY command in that it is more flexible, allowing various optional approaches to the process of copying files from one location to another.

• SWITCHES

/A   Adds files. Copies files from the source only if they do not already exist on the target. This option may not be used with the /S or /U options.

/P   Displays a prompt asking you to confirm each copy before copying the file to the target.

/R   Disables overwrite protection for read-only files on the target.

/S   Searches all subdirectories of the target directory for files that match the name of each source file. Source subdirectories are not searched. Do not use this option with the /A option.

/U   Updates only: replaces files in the target location only if they are older than those in the source location.

/W   Pauses processing before starting the replacement process. Allows you to switch source or target disks if necessary.

• EXAMPLE

REPLACE A:*.* C: /S /U /P

replaces files on drive C (the target) that have the same name as any files on drive A (the source)—if those files on drive C are older than the files on drive A—and prompts for confirmation before each replacement is made.

● ERRORLEVEL CODES

0 = Replacement successful

1 = Incompatible DOS version

2 = Source or target files not found

3 = Source or target locations not found

5 = Disk access denied; disk write-protect enabled

8 = Insufficient RAM for REPLACE

11 = Syntax error on command line

15 = Invalid drive specification

● **NOTE**   Do not use REPLACE to copy files from a source drive made using the BACKUP command from older versions of DOS. Use RESTORE instead. REPLACE does not work with hidden or system files.

See Also   COPY

RESTORE

E	!

Can overwrite or erase data!

Restores files from disks made using the BACKUP command from earlier versions of DOS.

• SYNTAX

RESTORE *source drive*: *target drive*:[*path**file(s)*] [*/switches*]

RESTORE requires two parameters: a source drive (a floppy-disk drive), where the backup files are located, and a target drive (usually a hard disk), where the restored files are to be located.

RESTORE is used only to restore files that were backed up using the BACKUP command. DOS 6 does not include a BACKUP command; this utility is present only for compatibility with earlier versions of DOS.

BACKUP remembers the original subdirectory locations of the files it backed up, and RESTORE restores the backup files to the same subdirectory. If the target subdirectory is not explicitly included on the command line, DOS assumes that the currently logged subdirectory is the target subdirectory. Therefore, before invoking RESTORE, be sure either to log onto the correct subdirectory or include the correct subdirectory path as part of the target parameter.

• SWITCHES

/A:*mm-dd-yy*	Forces restoration of only those files that were modified on or after the specified date, where *mm* is the month, *dd* is the day, and *yy* is the year. Files modified before the specified date are not restored.
/B:*mm-dd-yy*	Forces restoration of only those files that were modified on or before the specified date. Files modified after the specified date are not restored.
/D	Displays file name(s) on the backup disk but does not restore them. Notice that the target drive is still required in the syntax, although it is not used.

/E:*hh-mm-ss*   Forces restoration of those files modified at
                    or earlier than the specified time, where *hh*
                    is the hour (in 24-hour format), *mm* is the
                    minutes after the hour, and *ss* is the seconds.
                    This switch is effective when used with the
                    /B switch. Without a date parameter, target
                    files from different dates can be overwritten
                    if their time stamp matches the specified
                    pattern.

/L:*hh*:*mm*:*ss*   Forces restoration of only those files that
                    were modified at or after the specified time.
                    Files modified before the specified time are
                    not restored. Without a date parameter,
                    target files from different dates can be
                    overwritten if their time stamp matches the
                    specified pattern.

/M   Restores only those files that were modified
                    since the last backup was made.

/N   Restores only those files that were deleted
                    since the last backup.

/P   Prompts to confirm the restoration of files
                    that were changed since the last backup or
                    marked as read-only files. Without this
                    parameter, all files on the target drive with
                    names identical to the backup files will be
                    overwritten.

/S   Restores files in subdirectories nested below
                    the specified target subdirectory (or the cur-
                    rently logged subdirectory if no target sub-
                    directory was specified on the command line).

• EXAMPLES

RESTORE A: C:

restores those files from the backup disk in drive A that originally
resided on the currently logged subdirectory.

RESTORE A: C:\ /S /B:06-01-91 /E:13:00:00

restores files from backup disk in drive A to the root directory of drive C, plus all files below the root directory, except those on the target drive that were modified on or after June 1, 1991, at 1:00 p.m.

● ERRORLEVEL CODES

0 = RESTORE command completed processing normally

1 = No files were found to restore

3 = Command terminated prematurely with Ctrl-C from operator

4 = Command terminated prematurely because of some internal error

● **NOTE**   RESTORE does not work with system files.

See Also   MSBACKUP

SET

Creates environment variables and assigns values to them.

● SYNTAX

SET *variable name=value*

If you invoke the SET command without parameters, DOS displays a list of current environment variables and their values.

To initialize a variable or assign a new value to a variable, enter the name of a variable and an equal sign (=), followed by the desired value. The variable is stored in the operating system's *environment space,* an area of RAM set aside for this purpose. If the variable already exists in the environment, the value is changed to the indicated new value. If the variable does not already exist, it is created and assigned the value specified.

The environment space in DOS is limited. Refer to the SHELL command entry in *Appendix A* for details on changing the size of the environment space.

To remove a variable from the environment space, invoke SET with the variable name and equal sign, but do not indicate a value.

● EXAMPLE

    SET COMSPEC=C:\DOS\COMMAND.COM

assigns the string C:\DOS\COMMAND.COM to an environment variable named COMSPEC. DOS uses this system variable to remember the location of the file COMMAND.COM.

● **NOTE**   Many batch files and application software programs use environment variables. They can be quite handy. See *Appendix B* for examples of how environment variables can be used.

SETVER

Causes DOS to supply a different version number to an application.

● SYNTAX

    SETVER *drive:\path* application version */switches*

The SETVER command updates a table of applications that require DOS to provide an earlier version number. You must load this table into memory by including the command DEVICE=SETVER.EXE in your CONFIG.SYS file. Refer to *Appendix A* for details regarding the DEVICE command.

To display the current table of applications, invoke SETVER without the *application* or *version* parameters. To add an application to the table, invoke SETVER with the name of the application's executable file and the desired DOS version number. Thereafter, when you call that application, DOS will supply the specified version number rather than the current version. This is useful for programs that require an earlier version of DOS but can run under DOS 6.

● SWITCHES

/D	Deletes application names from the table.
/DELETE	Same as the /D option.
/Q	Suppresses on-screen messages when deleting applications from the table.
/QUIET	Same as the /Q option.

● EXAMPLE

SETVER OLDGAME.EXE 3.3

instructs DOS to tell the OLDGAME program that the DOS version number is 3.3.

● ERRORLEVEL CODES

0 = SETVER successfully completed

1 = Invalid command switch

2 = Invalid filename

3 = Insufficient system memory

4 = Invalid DOS version number

5 = Specified entry not in the version table

6 = SETVER.EXE file not found

7 = Invalid drive

8 = Too many command-line parameters

9 = Missing command-line parameters

10 = Error reading SETVER.EXE

11 = SETVER.EXE is corrupt

12 = Specified SETVER.EXE file does not support a version table

13 = Insufficient space in the version table

14 = Error writing to SETVER.EXE

● **NOTE**   Although the SETVER command will force DOS to provide a false version number, it does nothing to change the operating system's functioning. In other words, SETVER does not force DOS to act like an earlier version, but only to report that number. If an application requires exact version compatibility, you must use that version of DOS.

See Also   VER

SHARE

 E   TSR

Enables support for file sharing and locking.

● **SYNTAX**

SHARE /switches

SHARE is normally used on network systems, where the same application and data files may by used simultaneously. It prevents open disk files from being overwritten in ways that might compromise their integrity.

For example, if you open a file on a floppy disk, then switch disks before closing the file, SHARE displays an error message and temporarily suspends processing until you return the original disk to the drive.

If the SHARE command is invoked without option switches, default values for these switches are used.

● SWITCHES

/F:*nnnn*   Allocates space in RAM to be used to store the names of open disk files, where *nnnn* is the size of the storage space in bytes. The default is 2048 bytes.

/L:*nn*   Indicates the number of files that can be opened and locked at the same time. A file is locked when it is opened for reading or writing, and cannot be accessed until it is closed again. The default is 20 locked files.

● EXAMPLE

SHARE /F:4096 /L:32

activates the SHARE program, allocates 4096 bytes for file name space, and allows a maximum of 32 locked files.

● NOTES   If you have configured your hard drive to include partitions that are larger than 32Mb, SHARE is automatically loaded at boot time to assist DOS in handling the temporary files it creates to handle large disk partitions.

SHARE can also help prevent temporary files created by extended or expanded memory managers from conflicting with those created by application programs. Check the documentation for your memory manager and application software to determine if they recommend using SHARE.

SMARTDRV

E		TSR

Loads and analyzes the SMARTdrive disk-cache system.

● SYNTAX

SMARTDRV *drive+|drive-... /E:element size winsize /switches*

SMARTDRV is usually invoked in the AUTOEXEC.BAT file to enable the disk cache for all available drives at startup time. Floppy disk drives and Interlnk drives are read-cached but not write-cached; hard disk drives are read-cached and write-cached; CD-ROM, network drives, compressed drives, and RAM disks are ignored.

If you invoke SMARTDRV without parameters, all default settings are used. Optionally, you may override the defaults by supplying parameters and switches on the command line. Parameters are as follows:

drive   Specifies what type of caching is allowed for a particular drive, where *drive* is the drive letter. Notice that a colon is not used. You may specify any number of drive letters on the command line. Follow each drive letter with either a plus sign (+) or minus sign (–), or no sign at all, which will indicate one of the following:

+ = Enables both read and write caching
– = Disables both read and write caching
(no sign) = Enables read-caching only

size   Specifies the size of the cache (except when
            Windows is running). The larger the cache, the
            faster the performance, but the more memory is
            used up. Generally, you want to find a balance
            between the speed of the cache and the speed of
            your applications, based on their own memory
            requirements. The default value for this parameter
            is based on the amount of extended memory in
            your system (see *Notes*, below). If the default value
            slows your applications, try a smaller value for this
            parameter. You can determine the current size of
            your cache by invoking SMARTDRV without
            parameters and reading the screen display.

winsize   Specifies the smallest amount (in bytes) by which
            the cache will be reduced when you run Windows.
            This memory is released for Windows to use.
            When you exit windows, the cache is returned to
            its normal size. It is advisable to specify a value for
            winsize that is smaller than the value for *size*. If you
            specify zero, no caching is used when you run
            Windows.

• SWITCHES

/B:*size*   Specifies the size of the read-ahead buffer, in kilo-
            bytes. Its value can be any multiple of the *size* value
            supplied with the /E switch. Larger values require
            more conventional memory. Default is 16K.

/C   Writes all cached information from memory to
            the hard disk. Use this option before you turn
            off the computer to make sure all cached data
            has been written to the disk. When SMART-
            DRV is in memory, this option is invoked
            automatically whenever you press Ctrl-Alt-
            Del, but *not* when you power-off your
            computer or press the reset button.

/E:*Element*   Specifies the amount of the cache that
                SMARTDrive moves at one time, in bytes.
                Valid amounts are 1024, 2048, 4096, and 8192.
                Default is 8192. Larger values require greater
                amounts of conventional memory for the
                cache. Use this switch before any values you
                supply for the *size* and *winsize* parameters.

/R   Clears the existing cache and restarts
                SMARTDRV.

/L   Forces SMARTDRV to load into conventional
                memory. Try using this option if double-
                buffering is enabled (see *Notes*, below) and
                your system appears sluggish.

/Q   Disables status and error messages when
                SMARTDRV loads.

/S   Displays the current status of the cache.

• EXAMPLES

SMARTDRV a- b- 2048 1024

creates a 2048K cache, specifies that it will not be reduced by more
than 1024K, and disables caching on floppy disk drives A and B.

SMARTDRV /C

writes cached data to disks.

• NOTES   The purpose of the SMARTdrive disk cache system is
to speed up your system's disk operations. SMARTDRV automatically uses extended memory, provided that you have first installed
HIMEM.SYS (or a compatible extended-memory manager). If the
upper memory area is available, SMARTDrive will automatically
load into upper memory (unless you specify the /L switch). You do
not need to use the LOADHIGH command with SMARTDRV.EXE.

If you use EMM386.EXE or run Windows in 386 enhanced mode,
you may need to use SMARTDRV's double-buffering feature. To

enable this feature, include the following command in your CON-
FIG.SYS file:

```
DEVICE=SMARTDRV.EXE /DOUBLE_BUFFER
```

Include a drive and directory path if necessary, to enable DOS to locate SMARTDRV.EXE.

The default values for *size* and *winsize* are as follows, based on the
amount of extended memory in your system:

Extended Memory	*size*	*winsize*
0–1 Mb	All extended memory	0 (no caching)
1–2 Mb	1024	256
2–4 Mb	1024	512
4–6 Mb	2048	1024
6 Mb–Up	2048	2048

SORT

Sorts data in character-based files or sorts the output of DOS
commands.

● SYNTAX

SORT */switches* < *drive:\path\file*

Alternate syntax:

command **| SORT** */switches*

The SORT command will produce character-based output in
numeric or alphabetical order. It arranges individual lines in text

files, or each line of output. It is intended to be used on data lists (such as file directories or name lists) in which each line of the file contains some significant piece of information.

There are two ways to use the SORT command:

- If you would like to sort the contents of a data file, enter SORT followed by the redirection symbol for input (<) and the input file name. Wildcard characters are not allowed. SORT cannot handle files larger than 64K. SORT reads the file, sorts the lines, and displays the output. To redirect the output to another file, use the greater-than sign (>) followed by the output file name.

- If you would like to display the output of another command, enter the command and any required parameters followed by the redirection symbol for piping (|) and SORT. (Whenever you use a pipe symbol, you should first set a path name for an environment variable named TEMP, preferably in AUTOEXEC.BAT.)

You may also direct the command output that has been filtered through SORT to a file using the greater-than sign (>) and an output file name.

● SWITCHES

/R Sorts in reverse order (Z to A, 9 to 0)

/+*nn* Sorts using a character offset from the start of each line, where *nn* is the number of characters from the beginning

● EXAMPLES

SORT /R /+21 < NAMES.LST > RALPHA.LST

reads the file NAMES.LST, sorts it in reverse order on the 21st character of each line, and writes the result into a file named RALPHA.LST.

TYPE DATALIST.TXT | SORT

sorts the output of the TYPE command, displaying the contents of an ASCII file named DATALIST.TXT in alphabetical order.

• **NOTE**   Characters that are not alphanumeric will be sorted according to their ASCII table value. These values can differ among international character font sets.

SUBST

Associates a drive letter with a directory path. Drive letters used this way are called *virtual drives*.

• **SYNTAX**

SUBST *newdrive: drive:\existing path /switch*

To assign a drive letter to a directory, specify the drive letter that you want to use, followed by the directory path name. This drive letter cannot refer to any existing drive letter in your system. The highest default drive letter you can use is E. To use a drive letter higher than E, add the LASTDRIVE command to your CONFIG.SYS file. If you have added the LASTDRIVE command to CONFIG.SYS, you can use any drive letter up to and including the drive letter specified by LASTDRIVE. See *Appendix A* for details on LASTDRIVE.

The subdirectory path must already exist, and if the drive letter is different from the currently logged drive, it must be specified as part of the existing path parameter.

To display a list of current drive assignments, enter SUBST without parameters.

• SWITCH

/D   Deletes a drive letter that has been initialized with
      SUBST. Do not use the subdirectory path parameter
      with this switch.

• EXAMPLES

SUBST D: C:\WORD\USER\RUDOLPH

allows use of drive D in place of C:\WORD\USER\RUDOLPH in
all commands that reference this subdirectory.

SUBST D: /D

After invoking the previous example, this command deletes
drive D as a substitute for C:\WORD\USER\RUDOLPH.

• **NOTES**   The following DOS commands will not work on drive
letters that have been initialized using the SUBST command:
CHKDSK, DEFRAG, DISKCOMP, DISKCOPY, FDISK, FORMAT,
LABEL, RESTORE, RECOVER, and SYS.

The following DOS commands can work differently after SUBST is
invoked, and should be used with care to avoid confusion: AP-
PEND, CD, CHDIR, MD, MKDIR, PATH, RD, RMDIR.

Do not use the SUBST command while running Windows. If you
want to create or delete a virtual drive under Windows, first exit
Windows to DOS, invoke SUBST, then restart Windows.

To ensure compatibility with future versions of DOS, use SUBST instead of the (obsolete) ASSIGN.

SUBST, by allowing you to use a drive letter as a substitute for a
long subdirectory path name, can save you keystrokes. SUBST can
also allow programs that do not recognize subdirectory paths to
use them anyway via virtual drives. Because SUBST uses a single
drive letter for a long subdirectory path, it can also be used to ex-
tend the PATH and APPEND command parameters past their normal limits.

SYS

Copies DOS system files to a new disk.

● SYNTAX

SYS *source:\path* target:

SYS transfers the DOS system files (IO.SYS and MSDOS.SYS), plus the COMMAND.COM file, to a formatted disk without requiring reformatting.

You must specify a target drive where SYS is to place the operating system files. Optionally, you may include a source drive and path where DOS can locate the system files, before specifying the target. If you do not specify a source location, DOS looks for the files on the currently logged drive.

● EXAMPLES

SYS A:

copies system files to the disk in drive A.

SYS C: A:

copies system files to drive A from drive C, even if you are not logged onto drive C. The file *SYS.COM* must be available on the currently logged drive or the DOS search path.

● **NOTE**   SYS does not work on drives that have been reassigned using the SUBST command, nor will it work on a network.

See Also   FORMAT

TIME

Displays and allows changes to the system time.

● SYNTAX

TIME *hh:mm:ss.cc a|p*

If you invoke TIME without parameters, it displays the current system time and prompts you to enter a new time. If you do not want to change the current time, press Enter. Otherwise, enter the new time, where *hh* is the hour of the day in 24-hour format, *mm* is the minutes after the hour, *ss* is the seconds after the minute, and *cc* is hundredths of a second. Only the hours parameter (followed by a colon) is required to set a new time; other time values are optional.

If you include the desired time on the command line, the system time is changed without prompting you.

Time can be entered in 24-hour format, or 12-hour format. When entering a.m. time in 12-hour format, use the letter *a* after the time. When entering p.m. time, use the letter *p*. *A* is the default.

● **NOTE**   You can change the TIME format by changing the COUNTRY setting in your CONFIG.SYS file. For more information, refer to the COUNTRY command in *Appendix A*. Depending on the country code, MS-DOS will display the time in the 12-hour or 24-hour format.

● EXAMPLES

TIME 10:

changes the system time to 10:00 a.m.

TIME 22:30 TIME 10:30p

Either of the above examples changes the system time to 10:30 p.m.

See Also   DATE

TREE

Displays the subdirectory structure of a drive.

● SYNTAX

TREE *drive:\path /switches*

If you invoke TREE without parameters, the subdirectory structure of the current drive is displayed. If you include a drive letter, the structure of the specified drive is displayed. If you include a sub-directory name, the structure starting at the specified subdirectory is displayed.

● SWITCHES

/F   Includes the file names in each subdirectory.

/A   Displays the subdirectory using standard ASCII characters rather than graphic characters; this can speed up printing.

● EXAMPLES

TREE | MORE

displays the subdirectory structure of the currently logged drive, and pauses the screen display after each screenful of information.

TREE C: /F /A > PRN

displays the subdirectory structure of drive C, includes the file names in each subdirectory, and sends the output to the standard printing device in ASCII format.

● **NOTE**   The output from the TREE command can easily scroll off the screen, even when the subdirectory structure is relatively simple. For this reason, TREE's output is often redirected to a printer or a disk file, or piped through the MORE command. See the sections *Piping* and *Redirecting Output* in *Part One* and the MORE entry for more details.

TRUENAME

Displays the correct drive and subdirectory path names of drives and subdirectories that have been reassigned using the SUBST command.

● **SYNTAX**

TRUENAME *drive:\path*

When invoked without parameters, TRUENAME displays the correct name of the currently logged drive and subdirectory. When invoked with a drive letter, TRUENAME reports the true name of the current subdirectory of the specified drive. When invoked with a subdirectory parameter, TRUENAME reports the correct name of the specified path.

● **EXAMPLE**

TRUENAME E:

reports the drive and subdirectory path assigned to drive E.

See Also CD, SUBST

TYPE

Displays the contents of a file.

● SYNTAX

TYPE *drive:\path*\file

TYPE requires the name of a file. You may include a drive and sub-directory name if the file is not on the currently logged drive and subdirectory. Wildcard characters are not allowed in the file name.

● EXAMPLES

TYPE REPORT.TXT

displays the contents of a file named REPORT.TXT on the screen.

TYPE REPORT.TXT | MORE

displays the contents of the file and pauses the display after each screenful of information.

TYPE REPORT.TXT > PRN

sends the contents of REPORT.TXT to the standard printing device.

● NOTES
The TYPE command is intended to view ASCII text files. Program files and files created with many word processing programs may contain non-ASCII text characters and thus will not be readable using the TYPE command.

If the file displayed by TYPE is too large, it can scroll off the screen. For this reason, the output from TYPE is often redirected to a printer or piped through the MORE command. See the sections *Piping* and *Redirecting Output* in *Part One* and the MORE entry for more details.

UNDELETE

Recovers accidentally deleted files.

● SYNTAX

UNDELETE *drive:\path\file(s) /switches*

Invoke UNDELETE with the name of a deleted file. You may use wildcard characters to recover groups of files. If you omit a file name, UNDELETE will attempt to recover all the deleted files it finds.

For best results, invoke UNDELETE before any other information is written to the disk. Subsequent disk writes may overwrite the disk area occupied by the deleted file, making recovery impossible.

If you do not include a drive or subdirectory path before the file name, the currently logged drive and subdirectory are used.

UNDELETE displays each deleted file it finds that matches the specification in the command line. It prompts you to re-enter the first character in the file name, which was lost when the file was deleted. After you enter the characters, UNDELETE attempts to recover the file.

• SWITCHES

/S:*drive*

Enables *delete sentry* protection and loads the terminate- and-stay-resident (TSR) portion of UNDELETE. The program records information used to recover deleted files on the specified *drive*. If you do not specify a drive, the program records information on the current drive. If you have installed delete-sentry protection, you may use the /DS switch.

/T*drive-entries*

Enables *delete tracker* protection and loads the terminate- and-stay-resident (TSR) portion of UNDELETE. The program records information used to recover deleted files on the specified *drive*. If you do not specify a drive, the program records information on the current drive. The *entries* parameter specifies the maximum number of entries in the deletion-tracking file, PCTRACKR.DEL. Value for this parameter must be from 1 through 999.

The default value of *entries* depends on the type of disk you are tracking. Following are disk sizes, plus default value for *entries*:

Disk	Entries
360K	25
720K	50
1.2 Mb	75
1.44 Mb	75
20 Mb	101
32 Mb	202
32 Mb	303

Do not use deletion tracking for any drive that has been redirected using the SUBST command. If you intend to use SUBST, you must do so before you install deletion tracking. If you have installed delete-tracker protection, you may use the /DT switch.

/ALL

Invokes automatic undeleting and renaming of all specified files. Processing takes place automatically without prompts to the user to rename files. Files are renamed using a number sign (#) as the first character. If duplicate file names could result, UNDELETE supplies one of the following characters, in order, until it creates a unique file name:

#%&0123456789ABCDEFGHIJKLM NOPQRSTUVWXYZ.

/DOS

Forces UNDELETE to use the DOS file directory to locate and recover deleted files. This is the default when delete-tracker and delete-sentry protection do not exist.

/DS

Forces DOS to use the delete-sentry directory (if it exists) to locate and recover deleted files.

/DT

Forces DOS to use the delete tracking file (if it exists) to locate and recover deleted files.

/LIST

Lists all deleted files that may be recoverable.

/LOAD

Loads the terminate-and-stay-resident portion of UNDELETE into memory, using configuration information in the UNDELETE.INI file. If UNDELETE.INI does not exist, UNDELETE uses default values.

/PURGE [:drive]	Empties the delete-sentry directory. If no drive is specified, UNDELETE looks for the directory on the current drive.
/STATUS	Displays the type of delete protection in effect for each drive.
/U	Unloads the terminate-and-stay-resident portion of the Undelete program.

● EXAMPLES

UNDELETE *.BAK /LIST

lists all deleted files with the extension .BAK on the currently logged drive and subdirectory.

UNDELETE C:\WORD*.BAK

attempts to recover all files in the C:\WORD subdirectory that have the extension .BAK.

● NOTES Do not redirect the output of UNDELETE to a disk file. You may overwrite the files you are attempting to recover.

The results of using UNDELETE will vary from system to system. It is intended for last-resort use only. This utility is not intended to be a substitute for making backup copies of your files.

The delete-sentry protection method is the most protective of your files; it requires a small amount of RAM (13.5K) and some disk space. It works by moving deleted files to a hidden directory named SENTRY. If you undelete the file, DOS moves it back. The SENTRY directory is limited in size to about 7 percent of your total hard disk space. If the directory fills up, UNDELETE purges the oldest files until space has been freed to accommodate any newly-deleted file.

Delete tracker is slightly less protective, but requires a minimal amount of disk space. It records the location of deleted files in a hidden file PCTRACKER.DEL. You can undelete a file provided that another file has not been subsequently placed in the same location as the deleted one. Otherwise, you may undelete only a portion of the file.

The DOS directory method requires no additional RAM or disk space, but cannot undelete files reliably after disk writes.

If you do not specify a switch when you invoke UNDELETE, it tries to use delete sentry, followed by delete tracker. If neither protection method is available, it uses the DOS directory.

UNDELETE cannot restore a directory that has been removed, or files that were in a removed directory.

UNDELETE uses the UNDELETE.INI file to define values when UNDELETE is used. If the file does not exist when you invoke UNDELETE, it is created.

See Also   UNFORMAT

UNFORMAT

Recovers files from an accidental disk format.

● SYNTAX

UNFORMAT *drive*: */switches*

If a disk has been accidentally formatted, you may be able to recover files on it by invoking UNFORMAT (from a floppy disk, if your hard disk was reformatted), followed by the drive letter for the formatted disk.

• SWITCHES

/L	Lists all files and subdirectories found on the formatted drive
/P	Echoes program messages to the standard printing device
/TEST	Processes, but does not write any changes to, the formatted disk

• EXAMPLES

UNFORMAT C:

restores an accidentally reformatted disk in drive C.

UNFORMAT C: /TEST /L

tests recovery chances on a formatted disk in drive C when a FAT data file does not exist and lists file names found.

• NOTES   The results of UNFORMAT will vary from system to system. It is intended for last-resort use only. It is not an adequate substitute for backing up your data.

UNFORMAT cannot be used on a network.

If you formatted the disk using the /U switch, UNFORMAT cannot restore the disk.

If UNFORMAT finds a fragmented file (a file stored in noncontiguous sectors), it will recover only that portion of the file stored in the first sector. UNFORMAT prompts you to confirm whether you want to recover the truncated file or delete it. UNFORMAT may not be able to reliably recover all the files it finds. If information is lost or an executable file no longer runs correctly, you must restore the files from backup.

See Also   FORMAT, UNDELETE

VER

Displays the current DOS version number.

● SYNTAX

VER

The VER command displays the current DOS version. VER has no additional parameters or option switches.

VERIFY

Enables/disables the verify switch for writing files during DOS operations.

● SYNTAX

VERIFY *on/off*

If invoked without parameters, VERIFY displays the current state of the verify switch. Otherwise, invoke VERIFY using either the *on* or *off* parameter.

When the verify switch is on, DOS compares the image of a file just written to a disk with the image of that file in memory. DOS will display an error message if it is unable to write a verifiable copy of the file. When the verify switch is off, no such comparison is made. The default setting for the verify switch is off.

• EXAMPLE

VERIFY ON

turns on the verify switch.

• NOTES   Setting the verify switch on has the same effect on COPY commands as the /v option switch. Including this switch in COPY's command line overrides a verify off setting for the duration of the COPY command.

VERIFY has some limitations. The copy is compared to the image of the file in RAM, not the original file on disk. Thus, VERIFY will not discover any error that occurred while the original file was being read into RAM. The verification mechanism is a cyclic redundancy check, which only verifies that DOS wrote something to the disk. It is not a byte-by-byte comparison. To perform a more complete comparison of the file copy with the original, use the COMP or FC commands.

Displays the disk volume label.

• SYNTAX

VOL *drive*:

If invoked without parameters, VOL displays the currently logged drive volume label, if any. If you include the drive letter parameter, that drive's volume label is displayed.

● EXAMPLE

VOL A:

displays the volume label in drive A.

See Also   FORMAT /V, LABEL

VSAFE

 E   **NEW**   **TSR**

Monitors your system for the introduction of computer viruses.

● SYNTAX

VSAFE */options* +|– ... */switches*

Invoke VSAFE with one of the following *option* parameters to indicate how the program is to monitor for viruses. Follow the option number with a plus sign (+) to activate, and a minus sign (–) to deactivate:

/1   Warns of potential hard disk reformat (default: /1+).

/2   Warns of any program's attempt to remain resident (default: /2–).

/3   Prevents disk writes (default: /3–).

/4   Checks executable files on opening (default: /4+).

/5   Checks disks' boot sectors (default: /5+).

/6   Warns of attempts to write to hard disks' boot sectors or partition table (default: /6+).

/7   Warns of attempts to write to floppy disks' boot sector or partition table (default: /7–).

/8   Warns of attempts to modify executable files (default: /8+).

● SWITCHES

/A*key*   Activates hot key, as Alt plus keyboard *key*.

/C*key*   Activates hot key, as Ctrl plus keyboard *key*.

/D   Turns off checksum analysis.

/N   Allows network drivers to be loaded.

/NE   Does not monitor expanded memory.

/NX   Does not monitor extended memory.

/U   Removes VSAFE from RAM.

● EXAMPLE

VSAFE /2+ /7+ /CV

loads VSAFE, including all default settings, plus monitoring for any other program's attempt to remain resident in memory, any attempt of a program to write to any disk's boot sector, and activates the VSAFE display screen when the user presses Ctrl-V.

● NOTES   Do not install windows with VSAFE in RAM. If you run Windows while VSAFE is in RAM, add the following command to your WIN.INI file:

load=wntsrman.exe

WNTSRMAN allows windows to display VSAFE messages. Refer to your Windows documentation for details.

XCOPY

Selectively copies files.

• SYNTAX

XCOPY *source:\path*file(s) *target:\path\file(s) /switches*

At a minimum, the XCOPY command requires a source file name, which may include wildcard characters, plus optional drive letter and subdirectory path. You may provide a target parameter as well, which may be another file name, drive letter, subdirectory path, or a combination of the three. If you do not include a target, XCOPY will attempt to copy the source files onto the currently logged drive and subdirectory.

The source and target parameters may not duplicate the same file name and location. In other words, the XCOPY command will not copy a file onto itself.

If you use wildcard characters to indicate multiple source files and the target does not include a file name, copies of each file matching the source specification will be made in the target location.

If you indicate multiple source files and the target file name also includes wildcard characters, DOS will attempt to rename the target files in accordance with the wildcard conventions that you indicate. For predictable results, keep the wildcard character specifications consistent between the source and target file names.

• SWITCHES

The available options make XCOPY more flexible than the COPY command.

/A	Copies only those files matching the source specification that also have their archive bit set. See the ATTRIB entry for details about setting the archive bit.
/D:*date*	Copies files that were modified on or after the specified date. The exact format of the *date* parameter depends on the COUNTRY setting you are using.
/E	Creates subdirectories on the target location, even if there are no files in them. This switch is valid only when used in conjunction with the /S switch.
/M	Resets (turns off) the archive bit in a file after making the copy.
/P	Issues a prompt asking you to confirm the copy of each source file.
/S	Copies files matching the source specification that are found in subdirectories nested below the source subdirectory.
/V	Performs a verification check against the image of the file in memory.
/W	Causes XCOPY to pause before making copies, allowing you an opportunity to change disks in the source drive if necessary.

• EXAMPLES

    XCOPY C:\REPORTS*.TXT B:

copies all files in the C:\REPORTS subdirectory with the extension .TXT to drive B.

    XCOPY C:\REPORTS*.TXT B: /S /D:10/26/93

copies all files in the C:\REPORTS subdirectory, as well as any located in subdirectories nested below C:\REPORTS, with the extension .TXT, provided that they have been modified on or after October 26, 1993. The copies are placed on drive B.

● ERRORLEVEL CODES

0 = Copies made successfully

1 = No files found matching the source specification

2 = XCOPY aborted by operator (Ctrl-C)

4 = Invalid syntax on the command line or insufficient memory to run XCOPY

5 = Disk error encountered writing files

● NOTES   Unlike earlier versions of DOS, XCOPY in DOS 6 does not copy hidden or system files. XCOPY sets the archive attribute on copies it creates, whether or not this attribute was set in the source file. For more information about file attributes, refer to the ATTRIB command.

In addition to being more flexible than COPY, XCOPY can handle large numbers of files more efficiently, because it reads as many files as it can into memory before writing them to disk. This lessens the number of disk accesses. If you copy lots of smaller files, this can save you time and reduce disk wear and tear.

If you use the /A and /M option switches, XCOPY can copy a group of files that might not fit on a single floppy disk. Wait for the disk to fill up, replace it with a new disk, and restart XCOPY by pressing F3. Because the /A switch instructs XCOPY to copy only files with the archive bit set and the /M switch updates the archive bit after each file is copied, the earlier copies will not be included on subsequent floppy disks.

XCOPY has some advantages over DISKCOPY: fragmented source files will be defragmented on the target disk and XCOPY can copy files between disks with different data capacities. However, XCOPY cannot format disks on the fly as DISKCOPY can.

See Also   COPY, DISKCOPY

Appendix A

CONFIG.SYS Commands

The CONFIG.SYS file is an ASCII text file that contains instructions to DOS regarding your system configuration. It resides in the root directory of the default starting drive (drive C on most hard-disk systems or drive A on floppy-disk systems) and is read by DOS only once, at startup time.

Certain peripheral devices and applications require that you include commands in CONFIG.SYS. Other commands are used for such purposes as increasing disk-read buffers and the maximum allowed number of open files, loading peripheral device driver software, and increasing the number of logical drive letters in your system.

Because CONFIG.SYS is an ASCII file, you can edit it easily using a text editor or word processor that saves files in ASCII format. However, because CONFIG.SYS is read only at startup time, you must reboot your computer to activate any changes you make in the CONFIG.SYS file.

DOS 6 adds an important additional feature to CONFIG.SYS, the ability to display a menu of configuration choices and choose between them when you start your computer. This feature allows you to create alternate system configurations without modifying the CONFIG.SYS file each time. Rebooting is still necessary, however, if you want to switch settings during a session. Refer to *Part Two* for more details on defining multiple system configurations.

CONFIG.SYS commands are described in this appendix. For information regarding the standard device drivers supplied with DOS, refer to *Appendix C*.

With the advent of more sophisticated hardware systems, the order of commands in the CONFIG.SYS file has become increasingly important. If you are configuring your system to take advantage of memory beyond the normal 640K limit, be sure that you place any commands to configure this extra memory at the beginning of the

CONFIG.SYS file, before invoking any drivers or other software that utilizes this memory.

BREAK

Controls when DOS checks for Ctrl-Break entered by the user.

● SYNTAX

BREAK=*ON/OFF*

The Ctrl-Break or Ctrl-C key combinations cancel most DOS commands and some applications as well. Normally, DOS checks to see if the user entered Ctrl-Break or Ctrl-C only during functions that transmit data to and from the processor. BREAK=ON will cause DOS to check for cancellation during any DOS function call. This allows the operating system to cancel processing when commands or applications use very little data input and output.

You should avoid using BREAK=ON if applications have their own uses for Ctrl-C. The default status for BREAK is OFF.

● EXAMPLE

BREAK=ON

allows Ctrl-Break checking during any function.

BUFFERS

Sets the number of disk-read buffers.

● SYNTAX

BUFFERS=*##,n*

where ## is the number of buffers to be used by DOS. The valid range is 1 to 99.

A buffer is an area of memory set aside for temporary data storage. Buffers can speed up system performance by reducing the number of times DOS must directly access the disk; however, each buffer takes up about 530 bytes of RAM, reducing the amount of memory available for processing. Too many buffers will slow a system down.

Because computer systems vary so wildly, there is no hard and fast rule for determining the optimum number of buffers. DOS creates a default number of buffers based on the size of your RAM:

RAM Size	Default Number of Buffers	Bytes Used
Less than 128K (360K disk)	2	512
Less than 128K (Larger than 360K disk)	3	512
128–255K	5	2672
256–511K	10	5328
512–640K	15	7984

If you are trying to increase system performance by increasing the number of buffers, you might start with the following list, which relates buffers to the size of your hard disk:

Hard Disk Size (in MB)	Suggested Number of Buffers
20–32	20
40–80	30
80–120	40
120+	50

The *n* parameter specifies an additional number of *read-ahead buffers*, which store data just beyond the area of the disk being read, where *n* is the number of read-ahead buffers. DOS can anticipate up to 8 sectors of information on disk, so this number should be set to

8 in most cases. Read-ahead buffers further enhance system speed. Valid range is 0 to 8. Default is zero.

Read-ahead buffers can speed up your system if you are using an older, XT-style computer (8086 processor). If you are using a faster processor, install SMARTDRV.EXE or a third-party disk cache instead.

● EXAMPLE

    BUFFERS=30

installs 30 buffers.

● **NOTES**   If you are using a disk cache to enhance performance, check your documentation for recommendations regarding buffers. Some disk cache schemes (including SMARTDRV.EXE) require that you lower the number of buffers or eliminate the BUFFERS command entirely from CONFIG.SYS.

If DOS is loaded in the high memory area, it attempts to load the buffers there as well. If DOS is loaded in conventional memory, or there is not enough room in the high memory area, all the buffers are loaded in conventional memory.

COUNTRY

Installs international character sets and punctuation conventions.

● SYNTAX

    COUNTRY=code,*page*,*drive:\path\file.ext*

Use the COUNTRY command to start your system with a non–United States keyboard and display character set.

The *code* parameter is a three-digit number. If this command is not used, the default country code is 001 (the United States). The country code specifies the time and date formats used by the commands MSBACKUP, DATE, RESTORE, and TIME. The optional *page* parameter is a three-digit number for each code page number in the COUNTRY.SYS file. If this parameter is not supplied, a default is used for each country code.

Table A.1 lists country codes, default and alternate code pages, date formats, and time formats for countries supported by DOS 6.

Table A.1: DOS Country Codes

Country	Code	Default, Alt. Code Page	Date Format (Oct. 26, 1993)	Time Format (1 P.M.)
Belgium	032	850, 437	26/10/1993	13:00:00
Brazil	055	850, 437	26/10/1993	13:00:00
Canadian-French	002	863, 850	1993-10-26	13:00:00
Czecho-slovakia	042	852, 850	1993-10-26	13:00:00
Denmark	045	850, 865	26-10-1993	13.00.00
Finland	358	850, 437	26.10.1993	13.00.00
France	033	850, 437	26.10.1993	13.00.00
Germany	049	850, 437	26.10.1993	13.00.00
Hungary	036	852, 850	1993-10-26	13:00:00
International English	061	437, 850	26-10-1993	1:00:00.00p
Italy	039	850, 437	26/10/1993	13.00.00
Latin America	003	850, 437	26/10/1993	1:00:00.00p
Netherlands	031	850, 437	26-10-1993	13:00:00
Norway	047	850, 865	26.10.1993	13.00.00
Poland	048	852, 850	1993-10-26	13:00:00
Portugal	351	850, 860	26-10-1993	13:00:00

Table A.1: DOS Country Codes (continued)

Country	Code	Default, Alt. Code Page	Date Format (Oct. 26, 1993)	Time Format (1 P.M.)
Spain	034	850, 437	26/10/1993	13:00:00
Sweden	046	850, 437	1993-10-26	13.00.00
Switzerland	041	850, 437	26.10.1993	13.00.00
United Kingdom	044	437, 850	26/10/1993	13:00:00.00
United States	001	437, 850	10-26-1993	1:00:00.00p
Yugoslavia	038	852, 850	1993-10-26	13:00:00

You can also purchase special versions of DOS that support character sets for the following languages or countries: Arabic, Israel, Japan, Korea, People's Republic of China, and Taiwan.

The COUNTRY.SYS file is the default file for country-specific data. This file must be located on the root directory if the *file* parameter is not used. Include the *file* parameter if you are using a file other than COUNTRY.SYS or if the country-specific data file is not located on the root directory.

• EXAMPLES

    COUNTRY=002

installs the French Canadian character set.

    COUNTRY=002,,C:\DOS\COUNTRY.SYS

installs the same character set, and specifies that the COUNTRY.SYS file can be found in the C:\DOS directory. Notice in the above example that, when you omit the optional *page* parameter but include the file name parameter, you must still include the comma that follows the *page* parameter.

DEVICE

Installs device drivers.

● SYNTAX

DEVICE=*drive:\path\file* /*switches*

Many peripheral devices and some applications require that a special controlling software program, called a *device driver,* be loaded in memory. By convention, many device drivers have the file extension .SYS. DOS includes a number of device drivers, each with their own special options; refer to *Appendix C* for a discussion of these device drivers.

Use the DEVICE command, as instructed by your device driver documentation, to load the software program.

● EXAMPLE

DEVICE=ANSI.SYS

loads the extended keyboard and screen driver. Refer to *Appendix C* for examples of other DOS device driver syntax.

● NOTES   Some peripheral device drivers are contained in executable files that may be invoked from the DOS prompt. Be sure that your documentation specifies how your driver file may be loaded. DOS includes another CONFIG.SYS command, INSTALL, that permits you to load executable files from within CONFIG.SYS.

Not all files with the .SYS extension are device drivers. For example, do not use the DEVICE command to load COUNTRY.SYS or KEYBOARD.SYS. For information about COUNTRY.SYS, refer to the COUNTRY command in this appendix. For information about KEYBOARD.SYS, refer to the KEYB command in *Part Four*.

Check your driver instructions carefully to determine if a particular driver requires another driver be loaded first. Make sure the commands are listed in the correct order in your CONFIG.SYS file.

DEVICEHIGH

Installs device drivers in reserved memory, if space is available.

● SYNTAX

DEVICEHIGH /switches =drive:\path\file

If you include this command in CONFIG.SYS, you must have previously loaded the HIMEM.SYS device driver using the DEVICE command, plus an expanded memory manager that supports the Microsoft Extended Memory Specification for Upper Memory Blocks (XMS UMB, for short). An example of such an expanded memory manager would be the EMM386.EXE driver that is supplied with DOS. In addition, you must include the command DOS=UMB before using DEVICEHIGH. Refer to the DOS command in the following section for details. If you have not previously loaded these drivers, this command will function identically to the DEVICE command. Refer to *Appendix C* for details regarding HIMEM.SYS and EMM386.EXE.

Device driver files are normally loaded into conventional memory (0–640K) using the DEVICE command. The DEVICEHIGH command attempts to load the driver file into reserved memory (640–1024K) if it can find available space. Otherwise, the driver file is loaded in conventional memory.

All other syntax is identical to the DEVICE command. Refer to *Appendix C* for syntax examples of DOS device drivers.

● SWITCHES

/L:*region1,minsize1;*
region2,minsize2 …

Specifies regions of upper memory into which to load the program. If this switch is not used, DOS loads the program into the largest UMB it finds. Regions are numbered using integers beginning with 1. DOS loads the program into the largest UMB in the specified region, provided it can find a UMB that is larger than the program's load size.

You can specify more than one memory region in cases where a program uses more than one. Separate the region numbers on the command line with a semicolon.

Some programs expand in memory while running. If you are loading such a program, you can also indicate a minimum size for a UMB in the specified region (in bytes). DOS will load the program if it can find a UMB that is larger than the program's load size and the indicated minimum size. Separate the minimum size value from the region number using a comma.

/S

Shrinks the UMB to its minimum size while loading. This switch helps maximize use of upper memory. You can use this switch only if you are also using the /L switch to specify a minimum size for UMBs.

● EXAMPLES

Use the following sequence of commands before using DEVICE-HIGH (these examples assume that the driver files are located on the C:\DOS directory):

```
DEVICE=C:\DOS\HIMEM.SYS
DEVICE=C:\DOS\EMM386.EXE RAM
DOS=UMB
```

After using this sequence, the following syntax is valid:

```
DEVICEHIGH=C:\DOS\SETVER.EXE
```

which loads the SETVER.EXE program in upper memory.

If you use the MEMMAKER command to optimize your memory usage, MEMMAKER may add switches similar to the following:

```
DEVICEHIGH /L:1,12048 =C:\DOS\SETVER.EXE
```

● NOTES   Although the DEVICEHIGH command will conserve conventional memory, the required EMM386 expanded memory driver will take up about 5K of conventional memory. Therefore, this option is only practical if you have more than 5K of device drivers to load in reserved memory.

The DOS 5 syntax for DEVICEHIGH will still work with DOS 6, but it is not recommended.

DRIVPARM

Modifies disk drive parameters.

● SYNTAX

```
DRIVPARM=/D:drive /switches
```

The DRIVPARM command requires that you specify a physical drive connected to your system, using the /D: switch, followed by

a number indicating which drive is being reconfigured. Numbers are in the range 0–255, where 0 is drive A, 1 is drive B, 2 is drive C, and so forth. After specifying the drive to be reconfigured, use other switches to indicates the new configuration for the drive.

● SWITCHES

/C   Indicates that the drive is capable of detecting whether the drive door has been opened and closed.

/F:type   Specifies the drive type, where type is a number indicating the drive type. Valid values for type are:

> 0 = 180K or 360K (also 160K or 320K)
> 1 = 1.2Mb, 5.25"
> 2 = 720K, 3.5"
> 5 = Hard Disk
> 6 = Tape Drive
> 7 = 1.44Mb, 3.5"
> 8 = Read/Write Optical Disk
> 9 = 2.88Mb, 3.5"

The default for the drive parameter is 2

/H:heads   Specifies the number of read/write heads, where heads is a number in the range 1–99.

/I   Specifies a 3.5" floppy disk drive installed on your computer if your system's ROM BIOS doe not support 3.5" drives.

/N   Specifies a non-removable drive.

/S:sectors   Specifies the number of sectors per track, whe sectors is a number in the range 1–99.

/T:tracks   Specifies the number of tracks per side, wher tracks is the indicated number.

● EXAMPLE

DRIVPARM=/D:4 /f:6 /h:1 /s:80 /t:16

specifies that Drive E is a tape drive, uses 1 head, reads 80 sectors per track, and 16 tracks.

● NOTE   DRIVPARM is used to override the default settings for
data storage devices installed on your system. It should be used with special care, since invalid parameters will render drives unusable. Use this command in cases where a device is non-standard or the device's default configuration does not support the intended media type.

DOS

Loads the operating system in conventional, extended, or reserved memory.

● SYNTAX

DOS=*high/low* ,*umb/,noumb*

If you include this command in CONFIG.SYS, you must have previously loaded the HIMEM.SYS device driver using the DEVICE command. Refer to *Appendix C* for details regarding HIMEM.SYS. The UMB parameter is also required to use the DEVICEHIGH and LOADHIGH commands.

Use the HIGH parameter to load DOS into extended memory. By loading DOS in extended memory (that portion of RAM starting at 1024K), you can free a significant amount of system RAM for application software. You must have sufficient extended memory installed in your system to take advantage of this feature.

Use the LOW parameter to load DOS in *conventional memory* (memory between 0K and 640K). This is the default location for DOS if you do not include this command in CONFIG.SYS.

If you include the optional *UMB* parameter, DOS will attempt to load as much of itself as it can into *reserved memory* (that portion of RAM between 640K and 1024K). Any remaining part of the operating system will be loaded into memory as indicated by the HIGH or LOW parameter.

However, the UMB parameter is valid only if you have loaded an expanded memory manager that supports the XMS UMB allocation routines used by DOS; for example, the EMM386.EXE driver supplied with DOS. If you have not previously loaded such a driver, the UMB parameter has no effect.

You can force DOS to ignore upper memory blocks by specifying the *noumb* parameter in place of the *umb* parameter.

● EXAMPLES

    DOS=HIGH,UMB

loads DOS into reserved memory, with any remainder placed in extended memory.

    DOS=LOW,UMB

loads DOS into reserved memory, with any remainder placed in conventional memory.

● **NOTES**   This command is available only on 80386 or 80486 machines, and some advanced 80286 machines that are capable of mapping extended and reserved memory.

If you specify DOS=HIGH and DOS is unable to find or use the high memory area, it will display the following message:

    HMA not available
    Loading DOS low

FCBS

Specifies the number of open files using file control blocks.

● SYNTAX

FCBS=*maximum, open*

The FCBS command is used primarily with networking schemes that control the number of open files by means of *file control blocks*, which are pointers to the location of open files on disk. Include this command in CONFIG.SYS if you are using a network, the SHARE command, or software that manages open files by this method, if your software documentation instructs you to do so.

The *maximum* parameter indicates the maximum number of open file control blocks, from 1 to 255. Default is 4.

The *open* parameter indicates the number of files that will not automatically close if processing attempts to open more files than allowed by the maximum parameter. If processing attempts to open more files than allowed by the FCBS command, DOS displays an error message.

● EXAMPLES

FCBS=48,8

specifies a maximum of 48 open file control blocks, with up to 8 files protected from automatic closing if processing attempts to open more than 48.

FCBS=1,1

sets the maximum number of file control blocks to 1.

● **NOTE**   DOS 6 uses a different scheme of *file handles* for controlling the number of concurrently open files. This scheme is controlled by the FILES command.

FILES

Sets the maximum allowed number of simultaneously open files.

● SYNTAX

FILES=*n*

The *n* parameter indicates the maximum number of concurrently open files. Default is 8; maximum number is 255. If you exceed the maximum number of open files during processing, DOS displays the message "Too many files are open."

● EXAMPLE

FILES=25

indicates that a maximum of 25 files may be open at once.

● **NOTE**   Each increment to this parameter decreases the amount of RAM available to applications by 128 bytes; therefore, it serves no purpose to set this parameter any higher than the maximum possible number of files for your application. Refer to your software documentation to determine which one requires the largest number of open files, and set the FILES command to that number. You can experiment to determine the lowest practical number of open files on your system.

INCLUDE

Invokes a series of CONFIG.SYS commands from another section of the file.

● SYNTAX

INCLUDE=*block*

Use the INCLUDE command with a CONFIG.SYS file that contains multiple configurations. In a multiple-configuration CONFIG.SYS file, you can isolate and identify any series of commands that might be used in more than one configuration. Do this by listing the commands under a unique *configuration block name* in the file. Then, use this block name as the *block* parameter on the INCLUDE command line. Refer to the Example section just ahead for an example of this technique. Also refer to *Part Two* for more detailed information about multiple configurations.

● EXAMPLES

Following is an example of a simple block of configuration commands that might appear in a CONFIG.SYS file. Notice that the configuration block name appears within brackets:

```
[expanded-mem]
DEVICE=C:\DOS\HIMEM.SYS
DEVICE=C:\DOS\EMM386.EXE RAM
[exp-ramdisk]
INCLUDE=expanded-mem
DEVICEHIGH=C:\DOS\RAMDRIVE.SYS 1024 /X
```

Once this series of commands is so identified with configuration block names, a multiple configuration file that accesses the commands in the *exp-ramdisk* configuration block will access the commands in the *expanded-mem* block as well.

● **NOTE**   When first setting up your multiple configuration file, it may be easier to list all commands without using INCLUDE until the file is running properly. Later, you can condense the CONFIG.SYS file by gathering the duplicate command lines into a separate block and referencing that block with an INCLUDE command.

INSTALL

Loads terminate-and-stay-resident (TSR) software.

● SYNTAX

INSTALL=[*drive:\path*]*file.ext*

TSR programs are normally loaded by means of executable files at the DOS prompt. The INSTALL command lets you load TSR programs at the earliest point in the power-on process; this can help reduce conflicts by loading such programs in areas of memory where they are least likely to cause RAM addressing conflicts with other applications. Include a drive letter and subdirectory location if the executable file does not exist on the root directory. The file extension (.COM or .EXE) is required.

Four DOS external commands may be loaded this way: FAST-OPEN.EXE, KEYB.COM, NLSFUNC.EXE, and SHARE.EXE. Refer to *Part Two* for details regarding these commands.

● EXAMPLE

INSTALL=C:\DOS\SHARE.EXE

installs the SHARE command from the file located on the C:\DOS subdirectory.

● NOTES   This command speeds installation and minimizes addressing problems, but it will not prevent interrupt conflicts between TSR programs and applications. Some TSR programs permit you to unload them if they cause conflicts; in other cases, you may have to choose not to install TSR programs that cannot coexist with other software.

Some programs might not run correctly if they are loaded with the INSTALL command. Do not use INSTALL to load programs that use DOS environment variables (created using the SET command), or configure shortcut keys, or require that the command interpreter (COMMAND.COM) be already present in memory.

LASTDRIVE

Specifies the largest logical drive letter to be used by the system.

● SYNTAX

    LASTDRIVE=*drive*

The *drive* parameter is a letter from A to Z. The colon is not used in this syntax.

This command alerts DOS that you will be using more logical drive letters than actual logical drives in the system; for example, if you intend to use the SUBST command to assign drive letters to subdirectory names.

● EXAMPLE

    LASTDRIVE=H

sets a maximum of 8 logical drive letters.

● NOTES   DOS will set the highest drive letter automatically. You only need to use this command if your processing requires additional "dummy" logical drive letters, that is, more than the amount for which your system is configured.

Each additional drive letter over E takes up 81 bytes of RAM. You can save a little memory by setting no more than your actual upper limit of drive letters.

MENUCOLOR

Specifies text and background colors for a configuration menu.

● SYNTAX

MENUCOLOR=text,*background*

The MENUCOLOR command is used in a multiple-configuration CONFIG.SYS file to specify the text and background colors of the screen while a menu block is active. The *text* parameter is required. The *background* parameter is optional. The parameters are supplied as integers in the range 0–15, according to the following color codes:

Code	Color
0	Black
1	Blue
2	Green
3	Cyan
4	Red
5	Magenta
6	Brown
7	White
8	Gray
9	Bright Blue
10	Bright Green
11	Bright Cyan
12	Bright Red
13	Bright Magenta
14	Yellow
15	Bright White

● **EXAMPLE**

    MENUCOLOR=0,6

sets menu text as black, on a brown background.

● **NOTE** You can experiment to determine which colors you prefer on your system, but do not make the text and background the same, or the menu will not be visible. For more information regarding multiple-configuration CONFIG.SYS files, refer to *Part Two*.

See Also MENUDEFAULT, MENUITEM, NUMLOCK, SUBMENU

MENUDEFAULT

Specifies a default configuration block and optional timeout value for accessing the default.

● **SYNTAX**

    MENUDEFAULT=block,*timeout*

Use this command within a menu block in a multiple-configuration CONFIG.SYS file. The *block* parameter is required, and must be the name of a block of configuration commands that are identified elsewhere in CONFIG.SYS. The *timeout* parameter is an integer in the range 0–90, indicating the number of seconds DOS will display the menu before automatically selecting the default.

● **EXAMPLE**

    MENUDEFAULT=base,15

Indicates that the default is a block of commands identified elsewhere as *base* and that DOS will wait 15 seconds before automatically selecting this configuration block.

● **NOTE**   If you do use this command, DOS assumes the default is the first menu item. For more information regarding multiple-configuration CONFIG.SYS files, refer to *Part Two*.

See Also   MENUCOLOR, MENUITEM, NUMLOCK, SUBMENU

MENUITEM

Identifies a block of CONFIG.SYS commands to be included in a configuration menu.

● **SYNTAX**

MENUITEM=block,*text*

Use the MENUITEM command to identify available choices in a configuration menu in your CONFIG.SYS file. The *block* parameter is required, and specifies a block of configuration commands identified elsewhere in CONFIG.SYS. This block will be accessed if the user selects the indicated menu item. The *text* parameter is optional. It is a prompt that is displayed in the menu, detailing to the user the type of configuration that will be accessed if this menu item is selected. The prompt may be up to seventy characters long.

● **EXAMPLES**

The following example is a menu block with three menu items:

[menu]
MENUITEM=rdisk1,RAM disk (1024K)
MENUITEM=rdisk2,RAM disk (2048K)
MENUITEM=nordisk,No RAM disk

Assume that your CONFIG.SYS file contains configuration blocks named *rdisk1*, *rdisk2*, and *nordisk*. This menu block will then cause DOS to display the following menu when you start your computer:

MS-DOS 6 Startup Menu

=====================

   1. RAM Disk (1024K)

   2. RAM Disk (2048K)

   3. No RAM Disk

Enter a choice:

● **NOTES**   You may include up to nine menu items in a single configuration menu. If the specified *block* parameter does not exist in the CONFIG.SYS file, the menu item will not be included in the menu, and cannot be selected.

DOS automatically assigns numbers to menu items and displays them in the order they appear in the menu block. Unless otherwise specified with the MENUDEFAULT command, menu item number 1 is the default configuration.

For more information regarding multiple-configuration CONFIG.SYS files, refer to *Part Two*.

See Also   MENUCOLOR, MENUDEFAULT, NUMLOCK, SUBMENU

NUMLOCK

Turns the keyboard's numeric keypad on or off at startup time.

● **SYNTAX**

NUMLOCK=*ON/OFF*

Use the NUMLOCK command within a menu block in a multiple-configuration CONFIG.SYS file. The only valid parameter for the

NUMLOCK command is either ON or OFF. If set to ON, DOS turns the numeric keypad on when the menu is displayed. If set to OFF, DOS turns the numeric keypad off.

● EXAMPLE

NUMLOCK=ON

ensures that the numeric keypad is on when the menu appears.

● **NOTE**   The NUMLOCK command is a convenience command for systems that do not automatically turn the numeric keypad on at startup time. When NUMLOCK=ON, the user can use the numeric keypad to select CONFIG.SYS menu items. For more information regarding multiple-configuration CONFIG.SYS files, refer to *Part Two*.

See Also   MENUCOLOR, MENUDEFAULT, MENUITEM, SUBMENU

REM

Indicates a comment line to be ignored by DOS.

● SYNTAX

REM [*comment*]

The REM command allows you to place comments in CONFIG.SYS for documenting the purposes of commands, or refreshing your memory if you return to edit the file after a long period of time. You can also use the REM command to "comment out" certain CONFIG.SYS commands that you use only occasionally.

• EXAMPLES

REM The following loads the XMS extended memory controller

REM HIMEM.SYS (when the REM preceding DEVICE= is removed):

REM DEVICE=C:\DOS\HIMEM.SYS

The first two lines are a simple comment. On the third line, the REM command blocks loading of the HIMEM.SYS driver.

SHELL

Installs an alternate COMMAND.COM file and changes the environment size.

• SYNTAX

SHELL=[*drive:\path*]COMMAND.COM [*/switches*]

DOS looks for COMMAND.COM in the root directory of the drive used to load the operating system (drive C on many hard-disk systems or drive A on floppy-disk systems). Use the SHELL command to indicate a different location for COMMAND.COM; for example, you might put COMMAND.COM on a RAM disk to increase performance speed and reduce disk changes on systems without a hard disk.

If you are using a large number of environment variables in your system and run out of environment space, you can also use the SHELL command to increase its size. The default size of the environment space is 160 bytes; the maximum allowable environment size is 32,768 bytes.

● SWITCHES

/P   Loads the specified COMMAND.COM as the
            primary processor. Without this parameter, the
            specified COMMAND.COM is loaded as a
            secondary processor, and the EXIT command will
            return to the COMMAND.COM that was initially
            loaded.

/E:*nnn*   Indicates the size of the environment space, where
            nnn equals the size of the environment space in
            bytes; for example, 512 to indicate 512 bytes.

● EXAMPLE

SHELL=D:COMMAND.COM /E:512 /P

loads the copy of COMMAND.COM on drive D as the primary
processor, and increases the size of the environment to 512 bytes.

STACKS

Sets dynamic allocation of stack space.

● SYNTAX

STACKS=frames,size

Dynamic stack space allocation permits multiple interrupt calls to
call each other without crashing the system.

The *frames* parameter sets the number of stack frames. Default is 9,
except for IBM-PC, XT, or portable machines, where the default is 0.
Valid numbers of frames are from 8 to 64. The *size* parameter indicates the size of each frame. Default is 128, except for IBM-PC, XT,
or portable machines, where the default is 0. Valid frame sizes are
from 32 to 512 bytes.

● EXAMPLES

STACKS=18,128

increases the dynamic stack capacity to 18 frames, 128 bytes each.

STACKS=0,0

turns off dynamic stack allocation.

● **NOTE**   This command is generally not required, unless your application documentation calls for it. You may conserve memory on systems with tight RAM requirements by setting the STACKS parameters to 0. Increase the number of stack frames if you see the messages "Stack Overflow" or "Exception error 12."

SUBMENU

Specifies a submenu of additional choices within a menu block.

● SYNTAX

SUBMENU=block,*text*

The SUBMENU command is used within menu blocks in a multiple-configuration CONFIG.SYS file. The *block* parameter is required, and must be the name of a menu block defined elsewhere within the CONFIG.SYS file. This menu will be displayed if the user selects the indicated submenu. The *text* parameter is optional. It is a prompt that is displayed in the menu, detailing to the user what submenu will be accessed if this menu item is selected. The prompt may be up to seventy characters long.

● EXAMPLE

SUBMENU=alt-menu,Additional Configurations

will display an option to select a submenu block named *alt-menu* (provided it is defined in CONFIG.SYS), with the prompt, "Additional Configurations."

● **NOTES**   Submenus are useful if you have more than nine possible configurations, since any one configuration menu may have a maximum of nine possible choices. They may be useful in complex configurations where a hierarchical organization of options is desirable.

A submenu may contain its own definition commands for color and default. Unlike the startup menu, which must have the block name [menu], a submenu may have any menu block name.

For more information regarding multiple-configuration CONFIG.SYS files, refer to *Part Two*.

See Also   INCLUDE,   MENUCOLOR,   MENUDEFAULT, MENUITEM

SWITCHES

Allows backward compatibility from 101-key keyboards, movement of the WINA20.386 file from the root directory, and control of DOS startup options.

● **SYNTAX**

SWITCHES=/*switches*

Use the SWITCHES command with one or more of the available switch parameters to control various startup options.

● SWITCHES

/K   Causes the keyboard to emulate an older style, 84-key keyboard on systems with older programs that cannot recognize some of the keys on an enhanced 101-key keyboard.

/N   Disables function keys F5 and F8. When you include this switch, you cannot bypass startup commands.

/F   Disables the timed delay after displaying the message "Starting MS-DOS...." Use this switch to save a little time if you have also used the /N switch.

/W   Indicates that the WINA20.386 file does not reside in the root directory. Use this switch only if you are running Windows version 3.0 in enhanced mode. You must also inform Windows of the new location of WINA20.386 by adding the following command to the [386Enh] section of your Windows' SYSTEM.INI file:

device=*drive:\path*wina20.386

where *drive:\path* indicates the new location of the WINA20.386 file

Appendix B

Using Batch Files

A *batch file* is an ASCII text file containing a list of DOS commands. Each line in the batch file contains one DOS command plus any required parameters. In its most fundamental form, a batch file allows you to invoke a long series of DOS commands by entering a short command at the DOS prompt. This can simplify repetitive file management tasks and save you quite a few keystrokes.

Batch files can do more than this, however. Special DOS commands apply to batch files; using them, you can make batch files interactive, intelligent, and capable of performing highly complex file management tasks.

ASCII FILES

Batch files normally contain only those characters that you would create by typing: that is, letters, numbers, and standard punctuation marks. There are only a few exceptions to this rule, so if you are new to writing batch files, do not use non-ASCII control characters or high-order bit characters until you are completely comfortable with the basics.

DOS provides a useful, menu-driven text editor for creating and modifying batch files. To access the editor, invoke the EDIT command at the DOS prompt. For more details, refer to the EDIT command in *Part Four*.

If you are careful, you can create a batch file using most word processors, but you must be certain that you save the file to disk in ASCII format. Word processors refer to ASCII-format files by many different names, for example: DOS text files, ASCII files, Nondocument files, or unformatted files, among others. Consult the documentation for your word processor or text editor to determine how it creates and saves this kind of file.

If you are in doubt about whether you have saved the batch file correctly, you can display the file at the DOS prompt using the TYPE command. If invalid characters exist, they will appear on the screen as hieroglyphs (Greek letters, little smiling faces, and other strange symbols). If you find such characters in your batch file, there is a strong possibility that it will fail to run.

CREATING BATCH FILES FROM THE DOS PROMPT

You can create simple batch files from the DOS prompt using the COPY CON command. To do so, enter the following:

COPY CON *filename*.BAT

where *filename* is the name of the batch file you want to create. After you enter the command, the cursor will drop down one line and you may enter the commands you wish to include in the batch file. Each command, including any necessary command parameters, must occupy its own line in the file. Press Enter after each entry. The commands you enter will not execute, but the cursor will move to the next line.

Type very carefully! Once you press Enter, you cannot move the cursor back up to correct a previous line. If you make a mistake, your only recourse is to end the process and start over from scratch. For this reason, COPY CON is not recommended for anything but the shortest and simplest batch files.

When you have entered all your batch file commands, press **F6** or **Ctrl-Z**. The following symbol will appear on the screen: ^Z.

When you press Enter, DOS copies your commands into the file, and displays the message "1 file(s) copied."

BATCH FILE NAMES

Batch files can be given any valid DOS file name, but they always have the extension .BAT. When you enter the name of a batch file at the DOS prompt (not including the .BAT extension), DOS opens the file and executes the commands it finds just as if you had typed them yourself at the keyboard.

HOW BATCH FILES WORK

As an example of how batch files can save keystrokes, notice the following two-line command sequence. These commands are typical ones that you might invoke every day:

```
DEL C:\BOOK\*.BAK
```

XCOPY C:\BOOK*.* A: /M /S

The first command erases all the files with the .BAK extension from the C:\BOOK directory. The second invokes the XCOPY command utility to make a backup of files with the archive bit set in the C:\BOOK directory, including all subdirectories nested below C:\BOOK. The copy is made to Drive A.

If you like, you could create a batch file named FINISH.BAT, which includes similar commands that reference any drive letter or directory path on your system. Once you have created FINISH.BAT, you need only enter FINISH at the DOS prompt and DOS will execute the commands for you, thereby reducing over 40 keystrokes to just 7!

Many of the special batch file commands described in this appendix will improve the performance of even these two simple lines. Most of the examples in this appendix use variations on these two command lines to demonstrate the power of different batch file commands. If you like, you can substitute your system's drive letters and directory names and use these examples to demonstrate batch file programming to yourself.

AUTOEXEC.BAT

DOS makes use of one special batch file named AUTOEXEC.BAT. If this batch file exists on the root directory of the boot drive (drives A or C on most systems), the DOS commands in this file will execute automatically whenever the computer is started up or rebooted. This batch file usually contains special configuration and startup DOS commands, but it may contain any valid DOS or application command you want.

REPLACEABLE PARAMETERS

Many useful batch files do nothing more than slavishly execute the same series of commands each time they run. This is a perfectly acceptable use of batch files, but it carries a drawback: you must write a new batch file for any variation, no matter how slight, in the parameters of a command.

DOS allows you a greater degree of flexibility by permitting you to include up to 9 parameters on the command line when you invoke the batch file (more if you use the SHIFT command). These command line parameters are referenced in the batch file using the percent sign (%) followed by numbers 1 through 9 (0 is reserved for the batch file name itself).

For example, here is a variation on the FINISH.BAT file used above that includes replaceable parameters:

```
DEL C:%1\*.BAK
XCOPY C:%1\*.* A: /M /S %2
```

Having included %1 in the batch file commands in place of directory names, you may now supply the name of any directory path when you invoke FINISH. For example:

```
FINISH \BOOK
```

will invoke the commands using the C:\BOOK directory.

Although use of this technique means that you must enter an additional parameter on the command line, you have gained flexibility for your batch file, as it can be used on any directory path in your system, including nested subdirectories. For example, the following will also work:

```
FINISH \BOOK\CHAPTER3
```

will erase BAK files and backup all of the remaining files on C:\BOOK\CHAPTER3.

If you did not enter a directory name on the command line, DOS would replace the %1 parameter with nothing, and this would cause the commands in the batch file to reference the root directory.

The location of the replaceable parameters on command lines in the batch file is of critical importance. The %2 parameter used in this example allows you to add an additional optional switch to the XCOPY command. For example, you may want to execute this command more than once, adding additional backups to the existing ones, or you may want to start fresh with a new set of backup floppies. If you do not include a second parameter on the command line, DOS will read the XCOPY command and overwrite the disks currently in drive A. Alternatively, you could enter the following:

    FINISH \BOOK\CHAPTER /D:10-26-93

and DOS will make copies of the files dated 10/26/93, with archive bit set.

The percent sign can also be used to retrieve DOS environment variables (those variables initialized using the SET command) within batch files. To retrieve an environment variable, the variable name must be enclosed within a pair of percent signs. For example, the following batch file line, using the ECHO command, will display the setting of the COMSPEC variable:

    ECHO %COMSPEC%

Environment variables can be quite useful in batch files. For example, imagine that you are using the PROMPT command to send ANSI.SYS escape codes to the screen, but you want to save and return to the current prompt at any time. To do this, first create a batch file called NEWP.BAT that saves the PROMPT environment variable to a new variable, and changes the current prompt to whatever specification you provide when invoking it:

    @ECHO OFF
    SET SAVDPRMT=%PROMPT%
    PROMPT %1

In addition, you might want to include the SET command line in AUTOEXEC.BAT to be sure that this variable is always on tap.

Once you've saved a prompt, you can return to it anytime using a batch file called OLDP.BAT, which contains the following lines:

```
@ECHO OFF
PROMPT %SAVDPRMT%
```

Using NEWP and OLDP, you can save, change, and restore your prompt setting at will.

If a percent sign is not used in batch files according to the rules for replaceable parameters, DOS interprets it as a literal percent sign, for example:

```
ECHO Just a percent sign - %, nothing more.
```

will simply display the message exactly as it is seen here.

Many of the batch file commands in this appendix make use of replaceable parameters. Refer to the Examples section for each command for more demonstrations of their use.

BATCH FILE COMMANDS

The batch file command descriptions in this section enable batch files to make choices, perform repetitive tasks, call subroutines, and operate in various ways on optional parameters.

@

Suppresses the display of the line on the screen.

• SYNTAX

@ command

Command lines that include the @ symbol are processed normally, but are not displayed. This symbol must be the first character in the line.

• EXAMPLES

```
@ECHO OFF
DEL C:\BOOK\*.BAK
XCOPY C:\BOOK\*.* A: /M /S
```

suppresses the display of the ECHO OFF command.

• **NOTE**   The @ symbol is related to the ECHO OFF command. While ECHO OFF will prevent the display of all subsequent lines, this symbol prevents the display of only the line in which it appears. For this reason it is most often used with ECHO OFF to prevent that particular command from appearing on the screen.

: (COLON)

Indicates a section label in a batch file for use by the GOTO command.

• SYNTAX

:label name

In general, the legal characters for label names are the same as the legal characters for DOS file names, the one exception being that the period (.) is not used. Labels allow DOS to jump to any line in a batch file, using the GOTO command to reference a label positioned just before the target line. See the GOTO entry for details.

• EXAMPLES

```
:START
IF NOT EXIST C:\BOOK\*.* GOTO END
DEL C:\BOOK\*.BAK
XCOPY C:\BOOK\*.* A: /M /S
:END
```

will skip the DEL and XCOPY commands if there are no files on C:\BOOK (or if C:\BOOK doesn't exist) by jumping to the END label.

● **NOTES**   DOS allows you to put as many labels as you like in your batch files, and they may be of any length on a single line. However, only the first 8 characters in a label name are significant. Thus, labels named THIS_LABEL and THIS_LABOR are functionally the same.

When a label is encountered in normal sequential batch processing, it is simply ignored.

DOS does not require that you reference every label that you use. If you have used the ECHO OFF command in your batch file, you can use the colon as a substitute for the REM command; DOS will simply treat the line as a long label rather than a command line, and it will not ECHO the line to the screen.

CALL

Invokes a second batch file from within a currently running batch file, then returns to the original batch file.

● SYNTAX

CALL [*drive*:*path*\] *batch file*

CALL requires the name of another batch file. The .BAT extension is not required. You may include a drive letter and directory path if not the currently logged one.

● EXAMPLES

@ECHO OFF
CALL WP
DEL C:\BOOK*.BAK
XCOPY C:\BOOK*.* A: /M /S

calls WP.BAT, then returns to the batch file and invokes the remaining lines.

● **NOTES**   You may nest a series of called batch files several levels deep. DOS will allow you to CALL a batch file from within itself or have a file that was called call back the original calling file. However, it is up to you to avoid the possibility of an endless loop by including the proper command lines that will allow the batch process to end at the proper time.

If a batch file is invoked from within another batch file by name only, it will process normally, but will not return execution to the original calling file. This technique can be useful in cases where a batch file is making choices between several other batch files and you do not need to return to the original.

Do not use pipes (|) and redirection symbols (<, >, <<, or >>) with the CALL command.

CHOICE

Prompts the user for a response and sets the ERRORLEVEL variable based on the response given.

● SYNTAX

CHOICE /switches prompt

The CHOICE command allows batch files to be interactive and allows you to write batch files that are more flexible and "intelligent," choosing between alternate processing based on user input. CHOICE displays a prompt and waits for the user to press a key in response. Switches give you the option of specifying which keys are valid responses and allowing an automatic default response if none is given after a specified number of seconds.

The *prompt* parameter is a text string that the CHOICE command displays to the user. If you omit this parameter, CHOICE displays a default prompt based on the switches you have supplied.

• SWITCHES

/C:*keys*	Specifies the valid response keys, where *keys* is a character string representing the keys the user may press. When CHOICE pauses for input, these keys are displayed within brackets ([]), followed by a question mark. If you don't use this switch, valid response keys are Y and N.
/N	Suppresses display of the valid response keys.
/S	Forces response keys to be case-sensitive. Upper- and lowercase characters may be used in the /C:*keys* switch. Default is non–case-sensitive (DOS accepts either upper- or lowercase characters.
/T:*key,seconds*	Pauses for the number of seconds specified by *seconds*, and if no response is given, accepts the character specified by *key* as the default response. The *key* parameter must be a key specified in the /C:*keys* switch. The *seconds* parameter is a number in the range 0–99. If 0, CHOICE does not pause.

• EXAMPLES

The following example offers the user a simple Yes or No choice and defaults to No (ERRORLEVEL 2) if no response is given after 15 seconds:

```
@ECHO OFF
CHOICE /T:N,15 "Delete BAK files on C:\BOOK first"
IF ERRORLEVEL==2 GOTO MORE
IF ERRORLEVEL==1 DEL C:\BOOK\*.BAK
:MORE
XCOPY C:\BOOK\*.* A: /M /S
```

The following example displays a simple menu of options on the screen, and returns to the menu when each application is complete:

```
@ECHO OFF
:START
CLS
ECHO {W}ord Processor (WP.EXE)
ECHO {S}preadsheet (123.EXE)
ECHO {D}atabase (DBASE.EXE)
ECHO.
CHOICE /C:WSDX /T:X,15 "Choose an application, or X to exit"
IF ERRORLEVEL==4 GOTO END
IF ERRORLEVEL==3 GOTO DBASE
IF ERRORLEVEL==2 GOTO LOTUS
IF ERRORLEVEL==1 GOTO WP
:DBASE
DBASE
GOTO START
:LOTUS
123
GOTO START
:WP
WP
GOTO START
:END
```

• ERRORLEVEL CODES

The ERRORLEVEL values returned by choice depend on the number of valid key responses you have specified with the /C:*keys* switch. The first key in the string returns a value of 1, the second 2, the third 3, and so forth. If the user presses Ctrl-C, CHOICE returns an ERRORLEVEL value of zero. If an error occurs while choice is paused, it returns an ERRORLEVEL value of 255.

● **NOTES**   Evaluate the ERRORLEVEL values returned by CHOICE in descending order (highest possible to lowest possible). For more examples and information on evaluating ERRORLEVEL values, refer to the IF command later in this appendix.

If you want to use a forward slash character in the *prompt* parameter, enclose the entire prompt string within a pair of quotation marks.

See Also   IF

ECHO

Suppresses or displays batch file lines on the screen.

● SYNTAX

ECHO *on/off message*

The purpose of the ECHO command is twofold:

● To avoid cluttering up the screen with unwanted command displays

● To display custom messages on the screen to the user

If you invoke ECHO ON, DOS will display each subsequent line on the screen as it is executed. If you invoke ECHO OFF, the line display is suppressed. If you invoke ECHO without parameters, DOS displays a message indicating the current echo status.

If you invoke ECHO with any other character string, DOS will display the message on the screen, regardless of whether ECHO has been set ON or OFF.

You can use the ECHO command to skip a line on the display. To do so, use the following line:

ECHO.

which has the effect of displaying a null string. Notice that there cannot be any space between the ECHO command and the period.

● **EXAMPLES**

```
@ECHO OFF
ECHO Loading word processor...
CALL WP
ECHO Deleting BAK files before data backup...
DEL C:%1\*.BAK
XCOPY C:%1\*.* A: /M /S %2
```

displays the messages "Loading word processor..." and "Deleting BAK files before data backup..." before each command line. The command lines themselves are not echoed to the screen.

● **NOTES**   ECHO may be used to redirect character strings to a disk file or printer. This technique will work in batch files as well as from the DOS prompt. For example:

```
ECHO ^L > PRN
```

will send a form-feed to most standard printers, where ^L is Ctrl-L, not the caret (^) followed by L. You cannot display a pipe or redirection character using ECHO.

```
ECHO Send this character string to a file > TEST.FIL
```

will send the indicated string to a file named TEST.FIL.

FOR

Allows DOS to execute a command repeatedly.

● **SYNTAX**

```
FOR %%variable IN (dataset) DO command [%%variable]
```

The FOR command creates a condition called a *loop*, in which a single command is executed on a series of file parameters, until all parameters in the series are exhausted. In the above syntax, *dataset* is the series of parameters, *%%variable* is a symbol to be applied sequentially to each item in the data set and *command* is the DOS command to execute repeatedly, using each updated value for *%%variable*.

In other words, if this syntax were translated into plain English, it would read: "For each item in the indicated list, invoke the command, until you run out of items."

The IN and DO keywords are a required part of the FOR command. They must be positioned in the command line as shown.

For simplicity's sake, the %%*variable* name is usually a single letter, such as *A* or *X*. Do not use numbers as variable names, as DOS will mistake these for replaceable command line parameters. Variable names are case-sensitive. Do not mix %%*A* and %%*a* in the same command line.

The *dataset* parameter is always enclosed within parentheses. If the *dataset* parameter includes file names, wildcard characters can be used; every file that matches the specification will be included in the data set. For example, (*.*) would be a data set containing every file on the currently logged drive and directory.

• EXAMPLES

```
@ECHO OFF
FOR %%X IN (*.BAK *.OLD) DO DEL %%X
FOR %%X IN (*.*) DO IF NOT EXIST A:%%X COPY %%X A:
```

deletes all the files with .BAK and .OLD extensions. Then, it copies each file in the current directory to drive A, if that file doesn't already exist on drive A. In other words, the second FOR loop copies only newly created files, skipping those that were copied previously.

• NOTES
You can create a loop that moves through a list and executes a command without using the variable. For example:

```
FOR %%A IN (1 2 3 4 5) DO DIR /W
```

executes the DIR /W command exactly 5 times.

Although used most often in batch files, you may invoke the FOR command from the DOS prompt. If you do, use only a single percent sign in the variable symbol, rather than two. You cannot nest multiple FOR commands on the same command line.

GOTO

Redirects batch processing to the line immediately following the specified label.

• SYNTAX

GOTO *label*

The GOTO command allows different portions of the batch file to execute selectively. By combining labels, which are strings preceded by a colon, with GOTO commands, you can cause batch files to *branch* (skip over or execute specific lines depending on circumstances defined in other commands), or *loop* (repeat the same set of commands until a particular condition is met). For example, GOTO is often used with the IF command to jump to a specific set of commands when a particular logical condition is true.

• EXAMPLES

```
@ECHO OFF
IF NOT EXIST C:%1\*.* GOTO ERROR
DEL C:%1\*.BAK
XCOPY C:%1\*.* A: /M /S
GOTO END
:ERROR
ECHO Directory not found, or empty. Please try again.
:END
```

uses the IF and GOTO commands to determine if a correct parameter (in this case, a valid directory name, such as \DOS, or other directory on your system) was entered on the command line. If DOS cannot find files in the indicated directory (or the directory doesn't exist), GOTO ERROR causes the batch processing to skip the executable lines and jump to the part of the file that displays the error message. If the parameter was valid, the executable lines are invoked, and the GOTO END command skips the error message and jumps to the end of the batch file.

• **NOTES**   A GOTO command can skip forward or backward in the batch file. Using this command, it is possible to create an *endless loop* (a batch file that repeats without ever creating a condition that enables it to stop):

```
:START
DIR /W
GOTO START
:END
```

Under such circumstances, your only recourse is to terminate the batch file by pressing Ctrl-C.

Use the GOTO command carefully; it is wise to avoid complicated batch files that skip hither and yon. For best results, keep batch files straightforward and simple.

IF

Tests to determine if a particular condition is true. If the condition is true, executes a command. Otherwise, ignores the command.

• **SYNTAX**

To test a logical condition:

IF *condition command*

or:

IF NOT *condition command*

To test for the existence of a file:

IF EXIST *file(s) command*
IF NOT EXIST *file(s) command*

The *condition* parameter takes the form of an *equality test*, which compares two strings on the command line using two equal signs (==). For example:

IF "%1"=="/A" *command*

tests to see if the first parameter on the command line is /A. If it is, the condition is evaluated as true and the *command* following the condition is executed. If the parameter is anything other than /A, the condition is false, and the command is ignored.

The strings that are compared in equality tests are case-sensitive. Thus, in the above example, */A* would not be equal to */a*.

The quotation marks around the strings in the above example are not required for every equality test, but using them is good technique, especially when comparing replaceable parameters with literal values, as seen above. Quotation marks allow you to test whether a parameter was not entered; for example:

```
IF "%1"=="" command
```

would be true (and *command* would execute) if no parameter had been entered on the batch file command line. Without the quotation marks (or some extra character on both sides of the equality test) there would be no way to test for a null string. The following syntax has the same effect, but its meaning is less obvious since the exclamation point is less likely to be understood as a null string symbol:

```
IF %1!==! command
```

The condition parameter can also test for the value of DOS environment variables. For example:

```
IF %COMSPEC%==C:\COMMAND.COM command
```

returns true, executing *command*, if the COMSPEC environment variable is C:\COMMAND.COM. Notice that in this case, quotation marks are not necessary, although they could be added on both sides of the equality test if you like.

The condition parameter can also test for the value of *exit codes* that some DOS external commands (and a few third-party programs) store in the ERRORLEVEL environment variable.

When testing the value of the ERRORLEVEL variable, the condition will be true if the value stored in ERRORLEVEL is equal to or less than the value specified in the condition parameter. For example, if the ERRORLEVEL value is 1, both of these conditions would be true:

```
IF ERRORLEVEL==1 command
```

IF ERRORLEVEL==0 *command*

but this condition would be false:

IF ERRORLEVEL==2 *command*

Because of this peculiarity, if you want to test for several possible exit codes, start by testing the largest possible ERRORLEVEL value first, and move sequentially through the values until the lowest possible value is tested.

Finally, the IF command can test for the existence of files on disk, using the EXIST keyword. For example:

IF EXIST C:\COMMAND.COM *command*

would return true on many systems, since COMMAND.COM is often found in the root directory of a system's C drive. File names are not case-sensitive.

The NOT keyword reverses any logical condition evaluated by IF. For example:

IF NOT "%1"=="/A" *command*

returns true if the first parameter on the command line is not /A, or had not been entered. The condition will be false only if the first parameter is /A. (It will be true if the first parameter is /a.)

IF NOT EXIST C:\COMMAND.COM *command*

returns true if COMMAND.COM cannot be found on the root directory of drive C. If COMMAND.COM is there, the condition is false.

● EXAMPLES

Listing B.1 demonstrates several uses of the IF command. Line 2 causes processing to jump to the NODIR label if the operator failed to enter any parameters on the command line. Line 3 causes processing to jump to the ERROR label if the operator entered a nonexistent directory path or if no files were found. Line 4 will delete files with a .BAK extension, if any exist (thereby avoiding the confusing "File not found" message). Lines 6–10 test all possible values of the ERRORLEVEL variable and display an appropriate

```
@ECHO OFF
IF "%1"=="" GOTO NODIR
IF NOT EXIST C:%1\*.* GOTO ERROR
IF EXIST C:%1\*.BAK DEL C:%1\*.BAK
XCOPY C:%1\*.* A: /M /S
IF ERRORLEVEL=5 ECHO Command aborted.
IF ERRORLEVEL=4 ECHO Invalid syntax, or insufficient memory.
IF ERRORLEVEL=2 ECHO Ctrl-C detected.
IF ERRORLEVEL=1 ECHO No files were found to back up.
IF ERRORLEVEL=0 ECHO XCOPY completed normally.
GOTO END
:NODIR
ECHO Please specify a subdirectory path.
GOTO END
:ERROR
ECHO Directory not found, or empty. Please try again.
:END
```

Listing B.1: A batch file that demonstrates the use of IF

message in each case. The labels and GOTO commands assure that the batch file always branches to the appropriate executable lines.

● **NOTES**   IF commands can be nested on the same line. For example:

IF NOT EXIST *.BAK IF NOT EXIST *.OLD ECHO Not found

tests for the existence of files with a .BAK extension. If none are found, then it tests for files with an .OLD extension. If none are found, it displays the message "Not found." If files of either type are found, the message will not be displayed.

Nesting IF commands allows you to create complex logical conditions. However, you must be careful that your logic is entirely consistent. For example:

IF "%1"=="/a" IF "%1"=="/A" ECHO Parameter is /a or /A.

will never display the message, because these nested IF commands require the first parameter to be both /a and /A at the same time, which is impossible.

PAUSE

Pauses batch file processing and waits for the operator to press a key before continuing.

● SYNTAX

PAUSE *message*

The PAUSE command is useful when you would like to give the operator a chance to read a long message or to cancel the batch file before continuing.

When the PAUSE command is invoked, it displays the following message:

Press any key to continue...

If the user presses a key, the batch file continues. If the user presses Ctrl-C, DOS will prompt for the user to confirm cancellation before canceling batch processing.

The *message* parameter may be any character string. However, the *message* parameter will appear on the screen only if ECHO is set on and will include the PAUSE command itself, followed by the "Press any key" message. If ECHO is OFF, only the "Press any key" message appears.

You may customize the PAUSE message by preceding PAUSE with the ECHO command, echoing your intended message, then redirecting the PAUSE output to NUL.

● EXAMPLES

Listing B.2 shows a batch file that displays a two-line message indicating what is about to happen, then pauses the routine, allowing the operator to cancel or continue.

REM

Indicates that the line is a non-executable string, used to place explanatory remarks within the batch file.

```
@ECHO OFF
CLS
ECHO Will delete BAK files in, then back up, C:\BOOK.
ECHO Press a key to continue, or Ctrl-C to cancel the command.
PAUSE > NUL
DEL C:\BOOK\*.BAK
XCOPY C:\BOOK\*.* A: /M /S
```

Listing B.2: A batch file that includes PAUSE

● SYNTAX

REM *string*

The following syntax also works as a substitute for REM:

; *string*

The REM command allows you to include remarks in the file that explain what the file is doing. These remarks are helpful to others who read the file, or to yourself if you return to edit the file after a time and need to jog your memory. The semicolon is useful when remarks are many lines long, as the semicolon makes them a little easier to read. The semicolon must be the first character on the line.

Lines that begin with REM (or a semicolon) will display on the screen only if ECHO is set ON; otherwise, they are ignored by DOS.

● EXAMPLES

Listing B.3 shows a batch file that runs normally, but the included remarks are available to anyone who reads the file using a text editor or the TYPE command.

● NOTE   You cannot use a redirection character (> or <) or pipe (|) in a batch-file remark.

SHIFT

Shifts the location of command line parameters one position to the left, thereby allowing you to include more than 9 parameters on a command line.

```
@ECHO OFF
rem ** This batch file deletes BAK files, backs up what's left.
rem ** Requires a path name on the command line,
rem ** otherwise uses the root directory.
IF EXIST C:%1\*.BAK DEL C:%1\*.BAK
rem ** If a second parameter is included on the command line,
rem ** it must be a valid parameter used by the XCOPY command:
XCOPY C:%1\*.* A: /M /S %2
```

Listing B.3: A batch file that includes REM

• SYNTAX

SHIFT

The SHIFT command uses no parameters. Each time SHIFT is invoked, the parameters on the batch file command line are moved up one position; thus, the %9 parameter becomes %8, %8 becomes %7, and so forth. The %0 parameter is lost. If you have ten or more parameters on the batch file command line, the extra parameters are shifted as well. Thus, the tenth parameter will become the %9 parameter. Since only parameters %0 through %9 can be referenced within a batch file, SHIFT is the only means by which you may include additional parameters on the command line when invoking a batch file.

• EXAMPLE

Listing B.4 shows a batch file that performs a complex loop that allows you to erase .BAK files and make backups of any number of directories that you include on the command line, up to the limit of 127 characters on the command line.

• NOTES You cannot shift in reverse. Each time you execute the SHIFT command, the %0 parameter is lost. If you want to save the %0 parameter, store it in a DOS environment variable before you execute SHIFT. For example:

```
SET PARAM0=%0
SHIFT
```

```
@ECHO OFF
rem ** This batch file allows you to run the same two commands on
rem ** any number of subdirectory paths, by looping and shifting.
rem ** Remember to include a backslash (\) in front of each
rem ** subdirectory name on the batch file's command line.
rem ** STARTLOOP is the label for the top of the loop:
:STARTLOOP
rem ** Branch to ERROR label if current %1 parameter is bad:
IF NOT EXIST C:%1\*.* GOTO ERROR
rem ** Otherwise, process:
ECHO Now processing %1 directory --
DEL C:%1\*.BAK > NUL
XCOPY C:%1\*.* A: /M /S
rem ** ENDLOOP is the label to the bottom of the loop:
:ENDLOOP
rem ** This section shifts the parameters and then tests
rem ** to see if a %1 parameter still exists.
rem ** If so, processing branches to the STARTLOOP label:
SHIFT
IF NOT "%1"=="" GOTO STARTLOOP
rem ** If the above command does not execute, then all the
rem ** parameters have been used, so the file branches to the end:
GOTO END
rem ** Processing comes here if a bad subdirectory was entered:
:ERROR
ECHO %1 directory not found, or empty.
ECHO Press Ctrl-C to abort, any other key to skip...
rem ** Allows for early cancel:
PAUSE > NUL
rem **  starts over:
GOTO ENDLOOP
rem ** Processing comes here when all parameters are used:
:END
ECHO Processing complete...
```

Listing B.4: A batch file that demonstrates SHIFT

Appendix C

DOS 6 Device Driver Files

DOS 6 includes twelve standard device driver files for use in creating optional system configurations. These device drivers control memory allocations, display options, and disk drive usage. Different hardware manufacturers may license their own version of DOS 6 with other device drivers or drivers with syntax different than that listed here. If you are using another manufacturer's version of DOS 6, be sure to check their documentation for changes to the syntax described in this appendix.

The drivers in this section are all loaded into memory using the DEVICE command in the CONFIG.SYS file; except where otherwise noted, you may also load these drivers using the DEVICEHIGH command, provided that you have previously loaded HIMEM.SYS and EMM386.SYS.

ANSI.SYS

Extended screen and keyboard device driver.

● SYNTAX

DEVICE=*drive:\path*\ANSI.SYS */switches*

This driver loads extended capabilities for adapting the screen display and modifying the keyboard keys, to be used by applications that require these features. Consult your application's documentation to determine if it requires ANSI.SYS.

You may use the functions in ANSI.SYS to modify your screen and keyboard. Table C.1 lists the various ANSI Escape functions available once ANSI.SYS is loaded. Table C.2 lists the graphics mode and color codes. Table C.3 lists screen width codes. Tables C.4–C.8 list codes used to redefine keyboard keys.

Table C.1: ANSI Escape Sequences for Use in Batch Files

Function	Sequence	Parameter
Cursor to fixed position	ESC[*line;column*H	*line* = Cursor line number
		column = Cursor column number
Cursor to fixed position	ESC[*line;column*f	*line* = Cursor line number
		column = Cursor column number
Cursor up	ESC[*lines*A	*lines* = Number of lines up
Cursor down	ESC[*lines*B	*lines* = Number of lines down
Cursor right	ESC[*columns*C	*columns* = Number of columns right

Table C.1: ANSI Escape Sequences for Use in Batch
Files (continued)

Function	Sequence	Parameter
Cursor left	ESC[*columns*D	*columns* = Number of columns left
Display cursor position	ESC[6n	
Save cursor position	ESC[s	
Restore cursor position	ESC[u	
Erase display (Cursor to line 0, column 0)	ESC[2J	
Erase line from cursor	ESC[K	
Set graphics mode/color	ESC[*code;...;code*m	*code* = Mode/ color code(s)
Set screen width	ESC[=*code*h	*code* = Screen width code
Reset screen width	ESC[=*code*l	*code* = Screen width code
Redefine keystroke	ESC[*key;"string"*;p	*key* = Key code, *string* = New keystroke character(s)

Note: The letters ESC stand for the ASCII "Escape" character (Decimal 27; Hex 1B). Your text editor must be capable of producing this character to enter these sequences in your files.

Table C.2: ANSI Graphics Modes and Color Codes

Code	Meaning $Esc[... ; ... ; ... m$
0	Attributes off
1	Bold
4	Underscore (monochrome)
5	Blinking
7	Reverse video
8	Hidden
30	Foreground black
31	Foreground red
32	Foreground green
33	Foreground yellow
34	Foreground blue
35	Foreground magenta
36	Foreground cyan
37	Foreground white
40	Background black
41	Background red
42	Background green
43	Background yellow
44	Background blue
45	Background magenta
46	Background cyan
47	Background white

Table C.3: ANSI Screen Width Codes

Code	Meaning ESC [= ... h
0	Monochrome 40×25
1	Color 40×25
2	Monochrome 80×25
3	Color 80×25
4	Color 320×200
5	Monochrome 320×200
6	Monochrome 640×200
7	Word wrap on
13	Color 320×200 (graphics)
14	16-color 640×200
15	Monochrome 640×350
16	16-Color 640×350
17	Monochrome 640×480
18	16-Color 640×480
19	256-Color 320×200

Table C.4: ANSI Key Codes—Alphabet Keys

	x	*X*	Ctrl-*X*	Alt-*X*
a	97	65	1	0;30
b	98	66	2	0;48
c	99	67	3	0;46
d	100	68	4	0;32
e	101	69	5	0;18
f	102	70	6	0;33

Table C.4: ANSI Key Codes—Alphabet Keys (continued)

	x	*X*	Ctrl-*X*	Alt-*X*
g	103	71	7	0;34
h	104	72	8	0;35
i	105	73	9	0;23
j	106	74	10	0;36
k	107	75	11	0;37
l	108	76	12	0;38
m	109	77	13	0;50
n	110	78	14	0;49
o	111	79	15	0;24
p	112	80	16	0;25
q	113	81	17	0;16
r	114	82	18	0;19
s	115	83	19	0;31
t	116	84	20	0;20
u	117	85	21	0;22
v	118	86	22	0;47
w	119	87	23	0;17
x	120	88	24	0;45
y	121	89	25	0;21
z	122	90	26	0;44

Note: The first column lists the letters of the alphabet; the second column (x) shows the code that corresponds to each lowercase letter; the third column (X) shows the code that corresponds to each uppercase letter; the fourth column (Ctrl-X) shows the code that corresponds to each letter combined with the Ctrl key; and the fifth column (Alt-X) shows the code that corresponds to each letter combined with the Alt key.

Table C.5: ANSI Key Codes—Function Keys

	F*n*	Shift-F*n*	Ctrl-F*n*	Alt-F*n*
F1	0;59	0;84	0;94	0;104
F2	0;60	0;85	0;95	0;105
F3	0;61	0;86	0;96	0;106
F4	0;62	0;87	0;97	0;107
F5	0;63	0;88	0;98	0;108
F6	0;64	0;89	0;99	0;109
F7	0;65	0;90	0;100	0;110
F8	0;66	0;91	0;101	0;111
F9	0;67	0;92	0;102	0;112
F10	0;68	0;93	0;103	0;113
F11	0;133	0;135	0;137	0;139
F12	0;134	0;136	0;138	0;140

Note: The first column lists the function keys; the second column (Fn) shows the code that corresponds to each function key; the third column (Shift-Fn) shows the code that corresponds to each function key combined with the Shift key; the fourth column (Ctrl-n) shows the code that corresponds to each function key combined with the Ctrl key; and the fifth column (Alt-Fn) shows the code that corresponds to each function key combined with the Alt key.

• SWITCHES

/X   Enables keyboard redefinition features for duplicate keys on the newer, 101-key keyboards. This switch does not load ANSI.SYS into extended memory. Use the DEVICEHIGH command instead.

Table C.6: ANSI Key Codes—Number/Punctuation Keys

	n	Shift-*n*	Alt-*n*
0	48	41 ())	0;129
1	49	33 (!)	0;120
2	50	64 (@)	0;121
3	51	35 (#)	0;122
4	52	36 ($)	0;123
5	53	37 (%)	0;124
6	54	94 (^)	0;125
7	55	38 (&)	0;126
8	56	42 (*)	0;127
9	57	40 (()	0;128

Note: The first column lists the number keys; the second column (n) shows the code that corresponds to each number; the third column (Shift-n) shows the code that corresponds to each number combined with the Shift key, as well as the punctuation key associated with each combination; and the fourth column (Alt-n) shows the code that corresponds to each number combined with the Alt key.

/K   Ignores extended keys on 101-key keyboards. If you have used the SWITCHES=/K command in CONFIG.SYS, use this switch with ANSI.SYS.

● EXAMPLES

DEVICE=C:\DOS\ANSI.SYS /X

loads the full set of ANSI keyboard and screen redefinition functions.

The following examples show ANSI escape sequences that can be entered by means of batch files once you have loaded the ANSI.SYS driver. When you key in these examples, do not treat the letters *ESC* literally. They stand for the ASCII "Escape" character (Decimal 27, or hexadecimal 1B), which on some displays will look like a small arrow pointing to the left or a caret followed by a left bracket (^[). Be certain that your text editor can produce this character, and use it in place of the letters *ESC*.

Table C.7: ANSI Key Codes—Miscellaneous Keys

	K	Shift-*K*	Ctrl-*K*	Alt-*K*
spacebar	32			
–	45	95 (_)	31	0;130
=	61	43 (+)		0;131
[	91	123 ({)	27	0;26
]	93	125 (})	29	0;27
\	92	124 (	)	28	0;43
;	59	58 (:)		0;39
' (apostrophe)	39	34 (")		0;40
. (period)	46	62 (>)		0;52
, (comma)	44	60 (<)		0;51
/	47	63 (?)		0;53
` (rev. apostrophe)	96	126 (~)		0;41*
↑	0;72	56	0;141*	
↓	0;80	50	0;145*	
←	0;75	52	0;115	
→	0;77	54	0;116	
Del	0;83	46	0;147*	
End	0;79	49	0;117	
Enter	13		10	
Home	0;71	55	0;119	
Ins	0;82	48	0;146*	
PgDn	0;81	51	0;118	

Table C.7: ANSI Key Codes—Miscellaneous Keys (continued)

	K	**Shift-***K*	**Ctrl-***K*	**Alt-***K*
PgUp	0;73	57	0;132	
Pause			0;0	
PrtScr			0;114	
Tab	9	0;15	0;148*	0;165*
Null	0;3			

Note: The first column lists various keys; the second column (K) shows the code that corresponds to each key; the third column (Shift-K) shows the code that corresponds to each key combined with the Shift key; the fourth column (Ctrl-K) shows the code that corresponds to each key combined with the Ctrl key; and the fifth column (Alt-K) shows the code that corresponds to each key combined with the Alt key. Codes marked with an asterisk (*) are not available on some keyboards. To use these codes, install ANSI.SYS using the /X switch.

    ECHO ESC[34;46m

sets screen colors to blue letters on a cyan background.

    ECHO ESC[2J

clears screen after setting new colors.

    ECHO ESC[0;67;"COPY *.* A:"p
    ECHO ESC[0;68;"COPY *.* B:"p

redefines the F9 function key to invoke the command COPY *.* A: and the F10 function key to invoke the command COPY *.* B:.

Table C.8: ANSI Key Codes—Extended Keyboard Keys

Keypad Keys	K	Shift-K	Ctrl-K	Alt-K
/	47	47	0;142	0;74
*	42	0;144	0;78	
−	45	45	0;149	0;164
+	43	43	0;150	0;55
5	0;76	53	0;143	

Extended (Gray) Keys	K	Shift-K	Ctrl-K	Alt-K
↑	224;72	224;72	224;141	224;152
↓	224;80	224;80	224;145	224;154
←	224;75	224;75	224;115	224;155
→	224;77	224;77	224;116	224;157
Delete	224;83	224;83	224;147	224;163
End	224;79	224;79	224;117	224;159
Home	224;71	224;71	224;119	224;151
Insert	224;82	224;82	224;146	224;162
Page Down	224;81	224;81	224;118	224;161
Page Up	224;73	224;73	224;132	224;153

Note: These codes are not available on some keyboards. To use these codes, install ANSI.SYS using the /X switch. The first column lists various keys; the second column (K)shows the code that corresponds to each key; the third column (Shift-K) shows the code that corresponds to each key combined with the Shift key; the fourth column (Ctrl-K) shows the code that corresponds to each key combined with the Ctrl key; and the fifth column (Alt-K) shows the code that corresponds to each key combined with the Alt key.

DISPLAY.SYS

Loads international font sets for the screen display.

● SYNTAX

DEVICE=*drive:\path*DISPLAY.SYS
CON=(*type,codepage,additional,subfont*)

To specify an international character set using the DISPLAY.SYS driver, indicate a display type as well as at least one character set code page. The *type* parameter is one of the following:

EGA   Enhanced graphics adapter, also VGA displays

LCD   PC convertible adapter

The *codepage* parameter is a three-digit number representing international character sets. Valid numbers are:

437   United States

850   Multilingual (Latin I)

852   Slavic (Latin II)

860   Portuguese

863   Canadian-French

865   Nordic

The *additional* parameter is a number indicating how many extra code pages you intend to prepare using the MODE command. Valid numbers are in the range 1–6. Refer to the MODE command entry in *Part Four* for details on preparing code pages. Your system must be capable of handling multiple international character sets.

The *subfont* parameter is a number indicating how many subfonts your system supports for each code page. Default is 2 if *type* is EGA, 1 if *type* is LCD.

• EXAMPLE

DEVICE=C:\DOS\DISPLAY.SYS CON=(EGA,863,1)

loads the Canadian screen display font set and specifies that one additional font set will be prepared using the MODE command.

• NOTES
As an alternative to this driver, the COUNTRY.SYS and KEYBOARD.SYS files are also used to specify code page switching. COUNTRY.SYS is specified as a parameter to the NLSFUNC command; KEYBOARD.SYS is a parameter of the KEYB command that specifies several international keyboard layouts.

Code page switching is not supported for monochrome or CGA devices. You can specify CGA or MONO for the *type* parameter, but they have no effect.

DRIVER.SYS

Assigns logical drive letters to floppy disk drives.

• SYNTAX

DEVICE=*drive:\path*\DRIVER.SYS */switches*

Each time this command is invoked, DOS assigns the next available floppy disk drive letter to the specified device. The switches allow you to specify exact formatting requirements for the new logical drive. You can assign additional drive letters to the same or other devices by repeating this command in CONFIG.SYS.

• SWITCHES

/D:*n*   Indicates the drive number, where *n* is a number
from 0 to 127. 0 refers to the A drive, 1 to the B
drive, and so forth. Additional floppy disk drives
must be external. On a system with one internal
floppy disk drive, 0 refers to both drive A and B.
This switch is required and should be supplied
first.

/C   Enables change-line support, a feature that allows
DOS to detect if a floppy disk has been changed in
the drive during operations. Default is no change-
line support.

/F:*n*   Specifies the drive format, where *n* is a number
indicating one of the following formats:

    0 = 160K/180K or 320K/360K 5.25"
    1 = 1.2 megabyte 5.25"
    2 = 720K 3.5"
    7 = 1.44 Mb 3.5"
    9 = 2.88 Mb 3.5"

The default value is 2.

/H:*nn*   Indicates the number of heads per drive, where *nn*
is a number from 1 to 99.

/S:*nn*   Indicates the number of sectors per track, where
nn is a number from 1 to 99. Defaults depend on
the specified drive type, as follows:

    /S:9 = 360K and lower, 720K 3.5"
    /S:15 = 1.2Mb 5.25"
    /S:18 = 1.44Mb 3.5"
    /S:36 = 2.88Mb 3.5"

/T:*nnn*   Indicates the number of tracks on each side, where
          nnn is a number from 1 to 999. Default is 80,
          except for disks that are 360K and lower, in which
          case the default is 40.

● EXAMPLE

DEVICE=C:\DOS\DRIVER.SYS /D:1 /T:80 /S:9 /H:2 /F:2

assigns the next available drive letter to drive B, and indicates that it is to
be treated as a 3.5", 720K drive. Assuming that you have a system with
two floppy drives and a single hard disk, this command would allow
drive B to function as both drive B and drive D. Thus, you could copy
disks in the same drive by entering the command COPY B:*.* D:, and
DOS would prompt you to switch disks as required to make the copy.

● **NOTES**   DRIVER.SYS is intended for use by systems with external disk drive adapters and for systems that cannot normally copy
files from disk to disk on the same floppy-disk drive. You cannot use
DRIVER.SYS with hard disk drives.

The SUBST command also assigns new logical drive letters to existing drives and is usually easier to implement and understand.

If you are setting up RAM disks, place the RAM disk commands
after the DRIVER.SYS commands.

If you use the /F switch, you can omit the /H, /S, and /T switches
if default values are correct for the drive. If you specify the /H, /S,
and /T switches, you can omit the /F switch.

See Also   DRIVPARM (*Appendix A*)

DBLSPACE.SYS

Specifies the memory location of the compressed-data operating system driver named DBLSPACE.BIN.

● SYNTAX

DEVICEHIGH=*drive:\path*\DBLSPACE.SYS */switch*

DOS automatically loads DBLSPACE.BIN, along with the operating system, at start-up. Since it is loaded before other drivers that manage upper memory, it is initially loaded in conventional memory. Use the DEVICEHIGH command in CONFIG.SYS, along with the /MOVE switch, to move the compressed-data driver to upper memory.

● SWITCH

/MOVE Moves DBLSPACE.BIN from the top of conventional memory (its default location) to the bottom when used with the DEVICE command. Move DBLSPACE.BIN to the bottom of conventional memory to avoid conflicts with programs that require the top of conventional memory. This switch moves DBLSPACE.BIN to upper memory when used with the DEVICEHIGH command.

● EXAMPLE

DEVICEHIGH=C:\DOS\DBLSPACE.SYS /MOVE

moves DBLSPACE.BIN to upper memory. EMM386.EXE must be previously loaded for this command to work.

• **NOTE** Do not confuse these two similarly named driver files. Load DBLSPACE.SYS in the CONFIG.SYS file. This driver file only moves DBLSPACE.BIN. DBLSPACE.BIN is not loaded from CONFIG.SYS; DOS loads it automatically.

EGA.SYS

Driver which saves and restores EGA screens used with the DOS Shell Task Swapper.

• SYNTAX

DEVICE=*drive:\path*\EGA.SYS

This driver loads saving and restoring capabilities for EGA screens. Use this driver if your system has trouble handling screen displays when moving between programs in the DOS Shell. There are no switches and its functions are transparent to the user.

• EXAMPLE

DEVICE=C:\DOS\EGA.SYS

loads the EGA screen saver functions when the EGA.SYS file is stored on the C:\DOS subdirectory.

EMM386.EXE

Installs expanded and reserved memory support for 80386 and 80486 computer systems with extended memory.

● SYNTAX

DEVICE=*drive:\path*EMM386.EXE *size* ON/OFF/AUTO
RAM/NOEMS */switches*

The EMM386.EXE expanded-memory manager should be installed only after HIMEM.SYS (extended-memory manager) is installed. Do not load this driver using the DEVICEHIGH command. The DEVICEHIGH command is valid only after this driver is completely loaded.

● SWITCHES

size   Required only if you intend to configure a portion of your system's total extended memory as expanded memory, where *size* is a number indicating the expanded memory size in kilobytes (e.g., 64 equals 64K). If you leave out this parameter and the NOEMS parameter, up to 32768K (or the amount available on your system, whichever is less) of extended memory will be used as expanded memory. If you specify NOEMS, default size is 0.

A=*nnn*   Specifies the number of alternate register sets to use for multitasking, where *nnn* is the number of sets. The valid range is from 0 through 254. Default is 7.

AUTO

Loads the Expanded Memory driver, but activates the driver only when a program calls for expanded memory.

B=*nnnn*

Specifies the lowest address in RAM to be used as a bank for swapping portions of RAM to and from expanded memory. Valid addresses are from 1000 through 4000 hex. Default is 4000 hex.

D=*nnn*

Specifies the amount of memory to reserve for buffered direct-memory access, where *nnn* is the amount of memory in kilobytes. The valid range is 16–256. Default is 16.

FRAME=*nnnn*

Specifies the address in memory for the expanded-memory page-frame segment base, where *nnnn* is a number that specifies the base address in hexadecimal. Valid addresses are from 8000 through 9000 hex, and C000 through E000 hex, in increments of 400 hex. You can disable the page frame by specifying FRAME=NONE, although this is not recommended as it may cause some expanded-memory programs to work incorrectly.

H=*nnn*

Specifies the number of segment handles to be used, where *nnn* is the number of handles. The valid range is 2–255 handles. Default is 64.

I=*nnnn*–*nnnn*

Specifies a range of memory addresses to be used as page-frame addresses. Valid addresses are from A000 through FFFF hex, and are rounded down to the nearest 4K.

L=*nnnn*

Prevents a portion of extended memory from being used as expanded memory, where *nnnn* is the amount of extended memory to exclude.

M*n*   Specifies the address in memory for the
                        expanded-memory page frame, where *n* is
                        a number that specifies the base address
                        according to following:

                        1 = C000h
                        2 = C400h
                        3 = C800h
                        4 = CC00h
                        5 = D000h
                        6 = D400h
                        7 = D800h
                        8 = DC00h
                        9 = E000h
                        10 = 8000h
                        11 = 8400h
                        12 = 8800h
                        13 = 8C00h
                        14 = 9000h

                        Use numbers 10–14 on computers with at
                        least 512K of conventional memory.

MIN=*minsize*   Specifies a minimum amount of expanded
                        memory to be provided by EMM386.EXE,
                        if available, where *minsize* is the amount to
                        provide, in kilobytes. Valid range is 0
                        through the amount specified by the *size*
                        parameter. Default is 256, unless you
                        specify the NOEMS parameter, in which
                        case the default is zero.

NOEMS   Disables all expanded-memory support if
                        you have included the RAM parameter
                        and want reserved-memory support only.

NOHI   Prevents the upper-memory portion of
                        EMM386.EXE from loading into upper
                        memory. This switch increases memory
                        available for UMBs while decreasing
                        conventional memory.

NOVCPI   Disables VCPI application support. If you
                use this switch, you must also use the
                NOEMS switch. This switch reduces the
                amount of extended memory used by
                EMM386.EXE.

OFF   Loads but does not activate the Expanded
                Memory driver.

ON   Activates the Expanded Memory driver
                immediately upon loading. This is the
                default setting.

/P*nnnn*   Specifies the hexadecimal memory address
                for the page frame, where *nnnn* is a
                number that specifies the address. Valid
                addresses are from 8000 through 9000 hex,
                and C000 through E000 hex, in increments
                of 400 hex.

P*n*=*nnnn*   Specifies the page address, where *n* is
                the page number (0–255) and *nnnn* is the
                address in memory. Valid addresses are
                from 8000 through 9C00 hex, and C000
                through EC00 hex, in increments of
                400 hex. Pages 0 through 3 must be
                contiguous. If you use the M, FRAME, or
                /P switch, you cannot specify addresses
                for pages 0 through 3.

RAM=*start-end* Enables support for *reserved memory*, that
                area of RAM between 640K and 1024K,
                where *start-end* is a range of addresses (in
                hex) within this area. If you leave out the
                range of addresses, DOS looks for all the
                unused reserved memory it can find.

                When support for this memory is enabled,
                DOS will find and utilize unused portions
                of this area for loading other device drivers
                with the DEVICEHIGH (CONFIG.SYS)
                and LOADHIGH (command prompt)
                commands.

ROM=*start-end*	Reserves a range of memory addresses for shadow RAM, where *start* and *end* indicate memory addresses between A000 and FFFF hex. Address parameters are rounded down to the nearest 4K. Use this switch on systems that are not already equipped with Shadow RAM.
/V	Displays status and error messages during loading.
W=*ON/OFF*	Enables support for the Weitek math coprocessor if set to ON. Default is OFF.
WIN=*start-end*	Reserves a range of segment addresses for Windows, where *start* and *end* are a valid range of memory addresses. You may specify a range between A000 and FFFF hex. Ranges are rounded down to the nearest 4K. This switch takes precedence over the RAM, ROM, and I switches if the range specified here overlaps their ranges.
X=*nnnn–nnnn*	Excludes a range of RAM addresses for use as page-frame addresses. Valid addresses are from A000 through FFFF hex and are rounded down to the nearest 4K. This switch takes precedence over the I= switch if the two ranges overlap.

● NOTES

EMM386.EXE can be used only on computers with an 80386 or higher processor.

The /P*nnnn* and /V switches are the only switches that require the forward slash character.

Do not use EMM386.EXE switches frivolously. Normal defaults are established when switches are not used; use the default values whenever possible. EMM386.EXE can cause your computer to behave unpredictably if switches are used improperly.

If you are using Windows 3.1+, the I, X, NOEMS, M*n*, /P*nnnn*, and FRAME switches will override any settings for EMMINCLUDE, EMMEXCLUDE, and EMMPAGEFRAME settings in your SYSTEM.INI file.

Some systems may require SMARTDRV double buffering to transfer information into upper memory and expanded memory. Refer to the SMARTDRV.EXE section in this appendix for details.

● EXAMPLES

    DEVICE=C:\DOS\EMM386.EXE 1024 RAM

enables expanded-memory support for 1Mb of expanded memory, plus reserved-memory support.

    DEVICE=C:\DOS\EMM386.EXE RAM NOEMS

enables support for reserved memory only.

HIMEM.SYS

Loads extended memory support using Microsoft's XMS extended memory specification.

● SYNTAX

    DEVICE=*drive:\path*\HIMEM.SYS */switches*

Use HIMEM.SYS to enable extended memory support for all DOS commands that make use of RAM above 1024K. Such CONFIG.SYS commands include EMM386.EXE, DOS=HIGH, as well as any device drive that is loaded into extended memory.

• SWITCHES

/A20CONTROL:
ON/OFF

Forces HIMEM.SYS to assume
control of the *A20 interrupt handler* (that
portion of memory used to access
extended memory) at the time it is
loaded, when set to ON. When set to
OFF, HIMEM.SYS will assume control
of the A20 interrupt handler only if
it is not already being used when
HIMEM.SYS is loaded.

/CPUCLOCK:
[ON/OFF]

When set to ON, slows down
HIMEM.SYS on systems where the clock
speed changes when HIMEM.SYS is
loaded. Default is OFF.

/EISA

Forces HIMEM.SYS to allocate all
available extended memory on EISA
systems with more than 16K RAM. Not
required on other systems.

/HMAMIN=*nn*

Specifies the amount of memory an
application must use before having
access to extended memory, where *nn* is
the amount of memory in kilobytes.
The valid range is 0–63K. Default is 0,
meaning that HIMEM.SYS will allocate
extended memory to the first
application that requires it. This switch
has no effect when running Windows in
enhanced mode.

/INT15=*nnnn*   Specifies the amount of extended
                  memory HIMEM.SYS will ignore for
                  XMS support, where *nnnn* is a number
                  representing the amount of memory
                  in kilobytes. This switch allows
                  HIMEM.SYS to reserve a portion of
                  extended memory for use by programs
                  that require extended memory but are
                  not compatible with the XMS memory
                  specification HIMEM.SYS uses. Default
                  is zero. If you have applications that are
                  not compatible with XMS memory, set
                  this switch to the required amount of
                  non-XMS memory, plus 64K.

/MACHINE:*aaaa*   Specifies the type of CPU that you are
                  using to access the A20 interrupt
                  handler. *Aaaa* can be either a character-
                  based machine code or an equivalent
                  number, as indicated in Table C.9.

/NUMHANDLES   Specifies how many memory block
=*nnn*   handles can be used simultaneously,
                  where *nnn* is the number of handles. The
                  valid range is 1–128 handles. Default is 32.
                  This switch has no effect when running
                  Windows in enhanced mode.

/SHADOWRAM: Disables shadow RAM on some
ON/OFF   computers that support this feature and
                  adds the memory used by shadow RAM
                  back to available memory when set to
                  OFF. When set to ON, HIMEM.SYS
                  ignores shadow RAM. Default is OFF if
                  your computer has less than 1Mb of
                  extended memory.

/V   Displays status and error messages
                  during loading.

Table C.9: Equivalent Machine Code Numbers

Number	Machine Code	Description
1	AT	IBM PC/AT
2	PS2	IBM PS/2
3	PTLCASCADE	Phoenix Cascade BIOS
4	HPVECTRA	Hewlett-Packard Vectra A/A+
5	ATT6300PLUS	AT&T 6300+
6	ACER1100	Acer 1100
7	TOSHIBA	Toshiba 1600 and 1200XE
8	WYSE	Wyse 12.5Mhz 80286
9	TULIP	Tulip SX
10	ZENITH	Zenith ZBIOS
11	AT1	IBM PC/AT—Alternative Delay
12	CSS	CSS Labs (Also IBM PC/AT—Alternative Delay)
13	PHILIPS	Philips (Also IBM PC/AT—Alternative Delay)
14	FASTHP	Hewlett-Packard Vectra
15	IBM7552	IBM 7552 Industrial Computer
16	BULLMICRAL	Bull Micral 60
17	DELL	Dell XBIOS
18	KECARO	Keebler Elvin CARO

• EXAMPLES

    DEVICE=C:\DOS\HIMEM.SYS

enables XMS extended memory support for all available extended memory.

    DEVICE=C:\DOS\HIMEM.SYS /INT15=2048

enables XMS extended memory support for all memory, reserving 2048K for other programs not compatible with XMS.

● **NOTES**   Any DOS command that makes use of extended memory requires that HIMEM.SYS be loaded first. If you intend to use EMM386.SYS (or a compatible driver) to load support for expanded memory, you must load HIMEM.SYS first.

Do not load HIMEM.SYS with the DEVICEHIGH command. Use the DEVICE command instead.

INTERLNK.EXE

Directs instructions to drives or printer ports on the Interlink server.

● **SYNTAX**

DEVICE=*drive:\path*INTERLNK.EXE */switches*

Install the INTERLNK.EXE device driver on networked systems in order to use the INTERLNK and INTERSVR line commands. For details on these commands, refer to *Part Four*.

● **SWITCHES**

/DRIVES:*n*   Specifies the number of redirected drives, where *n* is the number. Specify 0 to redirect printers only. Default is 3.

/NOPRINTER   Disables printer redirection.

/COM*n*/*address*   Specifies a serial port for data transfer, where *n* is the number of the port (1–4). Alternatively, use the *address* parameter to specify the address of the serial port if it is non-standard. If you omit both parameters, DOS uses the first port it finds connected to the server. If you omit this switch as well as the /LPT switch, DOS scans all ports.

/LPT*n*/*address*   Specifies a parallel port for data transfer, where *n* is the number of the port (1–3). Alternatively, use the *address* parameter to specify the address of the parallel port if it is non-standard. If you omit both parameters, DOS uses the first port it finds connected to the server. If you omit this switch as well as the /COM switch, DOS scans all ports.

/AUTO   Attempts to establish a connection with the server when the client starts up. If no connection is made, INTERLNK.EXE is not installed. By default, DOS installs INTERLNK.EXE even when a connection is not made at startup time.

/NOSCAN   Disables attempts to establish a connection with the server when INTERLNK.EXE is installed. Default is to attempt to establish the connection.

/LOW   Forces DOS to load INTERLNK.EXE in conventional memory. By default, INTERLNK.EXE is loaded in upper memory if it is available.

/BAUD:*rate*   Forces maximum baud rate for serial
                      data transfer. Valid rates are: 9600, 19200,
                      38400, 57600, and 115200. Default is
                      115200.

/V   Ignores timer conflicts. Use this switch
                      with serial communications if data
                      transfers freeze the client or server.

● EXAMPLE

DEVICE=C:\DOS\INTERLNK.EXE /COM1 /NOPRINTER

loads the Interlink driver to use COM1 and specifies that printer
ports are not being redirected.

● **NOTES**   The location of the DEVICE=INTERLNK.EXE command in CONFIG.SYS affects drive assignments, especially RAM
disks. To prevent drive assignment errors, place the command last
in CONFIG.SYS.

If you are using a serial mouse with Microsoft Windows, specify
either the /LPT switch, or a /COM switch that designates a port
other than the one used by the mouse.

If you redirect LPT1 or LPT2 and print from Microsoft Windows,
use Control Panel to assign the printer to either LPT1.DOS or
LPT2.DOS.

Commands directed to another computer must be compatible with
the version of DOS the computer is running. The safest approach is
to run all computers with the same version of DOS, if possible.

The following commands do not work with the INTERLNK.EXE
device driver: CHKDSK, DEFRAG, DISKCOMP, DISKCOPY,
FDISK, FORMAT, MIRROR, SYS, UNDELETE, and UNFORMAT.

See Also   INTERLNK, INTERSVR (*Part Four*)

POWER.EXE

Lowers the rate of power consumption when devices are idle.

• SYNTAX

DEVICE=*drive:\path*\POWER.EXE ADV:*level STD/OFF /switch*

Use the DEVICE command to load this driver. The DEVICEHIGH command has no effect. By default, POWER.EXE attempts to load into upper memory.

Use the ADV: parameter to indicate your desired level of power conservation, where *level* is one of the following:

MAX   Conserves greatest amounts of power. Performance may be affected.

REG   Balances power conservation with performance. This is the default.

MIN   Conserves least amount of power, allowing near-full performance.

The STD parameter forces POWER.EXE to use the hardware's power-management features, if these features support the Advanced Power Management (APM) specification. If your hardware does not support APM, this parameter turns POWER.EXE off.

Alternatively, you can use the OFF parameter to turn off power management at startup time.

• SWITCH

/LOW   Forces DOS to load POWER.EXE device driver in conventional memory.

● EXAMPLE

DEVICE=C:\DOS\POWER.EXE ADV:MAX STD

loads POWER.EXE, allows maximum power conservation, and uses the hardware's power management features to respond to POWER.EXE's instructions.

● NOTE   Load POWER.EXE if your portable or laptop hardware has no built-in power conservation features or if you want to use the POWER command at the DOS prompt.

See Also   POWER (*Part Four*)

RAMDRIVE.SYS

Initializes a RAM disk.

● SYNTAX

DEVICE=*drive:\path*RAMDRIVE.SYS *size sectors directory /switch*

A RAM disk simulates a disk drive in RAM. RAM disks tend to be faster than physical drives, although the fastest hard disks can run almost as fast. RAM disks are also valuable when programs access the disk drive frequently, reducing drive wear as well as saving time.

RAM disks are volatile, however. You must save the data on a RAM disk to a physical drive before turning off the power to your computer. If you experience a power failure while running a RAM disk, all data that was not saved to a physical disk will be lost.

The *size* parameter indicates the storage area of the RAM disk, expressed in kilobytes. Default is 64, for 64K. The *sectors* parameter indicates the size of a disk sector, expressed in bytes. Default is 512 bytes. The *directory* parameter indicates the maximum number of directory entries, from 2 to 1024. Default is 64.

● SWITCHES

The following switches place the RAM disk in either extended or expanded memory. Use one or the other, not both. If you do not include one of these switches, DOS will place the RAM disk in conventional memory. If you install the RAM disk in extended memory, be sure to invoke DEVICE=HIMEM.SYS first. If you install the disk in expanded memory, load a compatible expanded memory manager, such as EMM386.EXE, first.

/A   Stores the RAM disk in expanded memory.

/E   Stores the RAM disk in extended memory.

● EXAMPLE

```
DEVICE=C:\DOS\RAMDRIVE.SYS 2048 512 1024 /E
```

installs a RAM disk in extended memory. Disk size is 2Mb (2048K); sector size is 512 bytes; maximum number of directory entries is 1024.

● **NOTES**   You can set up more than one RAM drive if you like, provided your system has sufficient memory to hold them. To set up additional RAM drives, repeat the DEVICE=RAMDRIVE.SYS command in CONFIG.SYS for each drive.

Many applications now make use of a TEMP environment variable, which references a disk directory. For maximum efficiency, set this variable to a directory on a RAM drive. If you are using Windows, use a RAM drive at least 2Mb in size to allow room for Windows' temporary files.

SETVER.EXE

Installs a list of software applications that require DOS to supply an earlier version number.

● SYNTAX

DEVICE=*drive:\path*\SETVER.EXE

The command to load the SETVER.EXE driver is automatically added to your CONFIG.SYS file when you install DOS 6. This command causes DOS to load a list of applications that require earlier version numbers.

You can delete this command from your CONFIG.SYS file if you are sure that none of your applications require an earlier version number. If you want to view or modify the list of applications, refer to the SETVER command in *Part Four*.

● **NOTES**   SETVER.EXE uses no optional parameters of switches.

In the CONFIG.SYS file, place the command DEVICE=SETVER.EXE before any DEVICE commands that load drivers requiring earlier version numbers.

SETVER.EXE only allows applications that require earlier DOS version numbers to receive their expected version number. Applications must be in all other ways compatible with DOS 6 to function correctly.

SMARTDRV.EXE

Installs double-buffering for a SMARTDrive cache.

● SYNTAX

DEVICE=*drive:\path*\SMARTDRV.EXE /DOUBLE_BUFFER

A *disk cache* improves system performance by storing the locations of frequently accessed files in memory, thereby reducing the overall number of disk accesses. The SMARTDrive disk cache provided with DOS 6 is normally loaded from the DOS prompt or from the AUTOEXEC.BAT file. For details, refer to the SMARTDRV command in *Part Four*.

However SMARTDrive can also perform *double-buffering*, which allows some hard disk controllers to work with SMARTDrive under expanded memory (as configured by EMM386.EXE) or when running Windows in enhanced mode. When double-buffering is required, this feature is loaded in CONFIG.SYS.

● SWITCH

/DOUBLE_BUFFER   Instructs DOS to use SMARTDrive's double-buffering feature.

● EXAMPLE

DEVICE=C:\DOS\SMARTDRV.EXE /DOUBLE_BUFFER

loads the double-buffering feature, assuming SMARTDRV.EXE is on the C:\DOS directory.

● NOTE   This command does not install the disk cache. To install the cache, refer to the SMARTDRV command in *Part Four*.

Appendix D

General DOS Error Messages

This section covers the error messages you are most likely to encounter while using DOS as a file manager or for configuring your system. The error messages in this section are related to problems that might occur through incorrect syntax entry, hardware error, and memory conflict with other software. The meaning of these messages is explained, followed by suggestions for solving the problem.

Not all error messages come from DOS; most applications have error messages of their own. If you receive an unfamiliar message while running an application, be sure to check the application's documentation for an explanation.

ABORT, RETRY, IGNORE, FAIL?

DOS failed to recognize an instruction it was given, or a disk or device error has prevented the instruction from being carried out. This message appears along with many of the other error messages in this appendix. You may choose one of four responses, as follows:

Abort   Press **A** to terminate the program entirely and return to the DOS prompt.

Retry   Press **R** to repeat the instruction. This works in cases where you can make a change in the system (for example, closing a disk-drive door), or when a momentary pause will allow a conflict to resolve itself (for example, waiting for the printer to warm up and come on-line). If you press R a few times and continue to receive this message, press A.

Ignore   Press **I** to continue with processing, as if the error had not occurred. This option is risky, and is not recommended unless you are a software developer testing a program or are absolutely certain that continued processing will not have destructive results.

Fail   Press **F** to cancel the problematic instruction but continue with processing. Like Ignore, this is a risky option, because ignoring this instruction can cause unexpected results later on. Use it only if you know for certain what will happen.

ACCESS DENIED

You attempted to open a file that is either labeled read-only, stored on a write-protected disk, or locked on a network. This message also appears if you use the TYPE command on a subdirectory or the CD or CHDIR command on a file. Use the ATTRIB command to remove the file's read-only status, remove the write protection from the disk, or change the file name specification, and then try again.

ACTIVE CODE PAGE NOT AVAILABLE

The desired code page is not valid for the display device you are using. Use a different code page number.

ALL FILES IN DIRECTORY WILL BE DELETED! ARE YOU SURE?

You are about to delete all the files in the specified directory or the currently logged directory. Enter Y if you intend to do this; otherwise, enter N.

ANSI.SYS MUST BE INSTALLED

You have neglected to install ANSI.SYS or have not used the correct syntax in the CONFIG.SYS file. Check the syntax in CONFIG.SYS and reboot the computer.

ATTEMPT TO REMOVE CURRENT DIRECTORY

You invoked the RD or RMDIR commands using the name of the currently logged directory. Log onto the parent directory and try again. You cannot remove the root directory.

BAD COMMAND OR FILE NAME

DOS did not recognize the command you entered at the DOS prompt. Check to make sure that you have entered the command correctly and that the command file can be found either on the specified directory or on the search path indicated by the PATH command.

BAD EXTENDED MEMORY MANAGER CONTROL CHAIN

A device driver is in conflict with another driver in the CON-FIG.SYS file. Remove all installable drivers that come before the problem driver, except HIMEM.SYS, and re-install them one by one until the error message reappears. You must reboot your computer each time. Do not use the offending driver with the current driver.

BAD OR MISSING COMMAND INTERPRETER

You have attempted to load a version of COMMAND.COM that is not compatible with the current operating system, or COMMAND.COM cannot be found. Reboot, using a bootable floppy disk if necessary. Check that the correct version of COMMAND.COM is on the root directory, and that the correct version of COMMAND.COM has been specified using the SHELL command in CONFIG.SYS. Refer to the Format command in *Part Four* for details on creating a bootable floppy disk.

BAD OR MISSING *DRIVER*

DOS cannot locate the device driver file, or the file has become corrupted. Copy the driver file from backup onto the root directory or specify the location of the file on the initialization line in CONFIG.SYS.

BAD OR MISSING KEYBOARD DEFINITION FILE

DOS could not find the KEYBOARD.SYS file, or it has become corrupted. Be sure that KEYBOARD.SYS is located on the same directory as KEYB.EXE. If necessary, copy a new KEYBOARD.SYS file from backup.

BAD UMB NUMBER

An application has referenced an invalid Upper Memory Block address. If you receive this message at startup time, try running MEMMAKER to correct the problem. If necessary reboot using the **F8** function key to bypass CONFIG.SYS and AUTOEXEC.BAT. If you receive this message when using the LH or LOADHIGH commands, remove the /L switch and its accompanying parameters. This message may also indicate a memory addressing problem requiring hardware service.

BATCH FILE MISSING

Usually this message appears after a batch file has erased itself. Rewrite the batch file or restore it using the UNDELETE command. Edit the batch file, using extra care with batch file commands that delete files, especially if they include wildcard parameters.

BOOT ERROR

DOS was not able to detect the presence of the expected peripheral devices at boot time. Check your computer's setup parameters using your system's setup utility. If necessary, perform a low-level format and repartition the disk drive. If you cannot solve the problem yourself, have the computer serviced by a professional diagnostician.

CANNOT CHDIR TO PATH

·CHKDSK cannot verify the existence of a subdirectory reported in the FAT. Run CHKDSK with the /F option to correct the problem.

CANNOT CHDIR TO ROOT

CHKDSK cannot locate the start of the root directory. Reboot the computer and re-invoke the command. If the problem continues, back up what files you can, if any, and reformat the disk.

CANNOT DO BINARY READS FROM A DEVICE

Do not specify the /B option when using the COPY command to copy to or from this peripheral device. If necessary, use the /A option to force an ASCII copy.

CANNOT FIND SYSTEM FILES

You have attempted to load the operating system from a drive that does not contain system files. Use the SYS command to copy the system files to the drive and restore backup copies of CONFIG.SYS and AUTOEXEC.BAT to the root directory if necessary. If you cannot restore the system files, boot from a floppy disk, backup your data, and reformat the disk using the FORMAT /S command.

CANNOT LOAD COMMAND, SYSTEM HALTED

An application has overwritten all or part of COMMAND.COM in memory, and DOS is unable to reload the command processor. Another possibility it that the COMSPEC environment variable has been reset to a nonexistent path name for COMMAND.COM. Reboot the computer, using the **F8** function key if necessary. Check the integrity of the data modified by the application. If necessary, copy COMMAND.COM to another directory and set the COMSPEC variable to that directory in AUTOEXEC.BAT.

CANNOT LOADHIGH BATCH FILE

Do not attempt to use the LOADHIGH or LH commands to run a batch file. This may happen in batch files using replaceable parameters for command names. Avoid using batch files with the same name as executable files.

CANNOT OPEN SPECIFIED COUNTRY INFORMATION FILE

You have used an invalid file name for country code pages in CONFIG.SYS. If you see this message at startup, check the syntax of the COUNTRY command in CONFIG.SYS, as well as the NLSFUNC, KEYB, and MODE commands in AUTOEXEC.BAT.

CANNOT PERFORM A CYCLIC COPY

You have attempted to copy files onto themselves. This can happen when use XCOPY with the /S option and are attempting to copy to a subdirectory nested below the source subdirectory. Use caution when specifying wildcard characters. Correct the syntax and try again.

CANNOT READ FILE ALLOCATION TABLE

The file allocation table has become corrupted. If you can still find some of your data, back up whatever you can find onto blank diskettes. Do not overwrite any previous backups. You may be able to repair the file allocation table using the CHKDSK command. If necessary, reformat the disk. If the problem occurs repeatedly, have the drive serviced or replaced.

CANNOT SETUP EXPANDED MEMORY

EMM386.EXE cannot initialize properly. Check the syntax of the initialization line in CONFIG.SYS. Be certain that HIMEM.SYS is installed before the memory manager. If necessary, have your system memory tested and serviced.

CANNOT START COMMAND

See the "Cannot load COMMAND" error message entry.

CODE PAGE DRIVE CANNOT BE INITIALIZED

You may have included an invalid parameter in the code page driver initialization line. Edit CONFIG.SYS and correct the syntax, then reboot the computer.

CODE PAGE OPERATION NOT SUPPORTED

You have entered an invalid code page combination, or one that cannot be used on the currently installed device. Check the validity of your code page parameters and re-invoke the command. Refer to the MODE and NLSFUNC commands in *Part Four* and the COUNTRY command in *Appendix A* for details on preparing code pages.

CODE PAGE NOT PREPARED

You have referenced a code page number that was not previously prepared using the MODE command. Refer to the MODE and

NLSFUNC commands in *Part Four* and the COUNTRY command in *Appendix A* for details on preparing code pages.

CODE PAGE MISMATCH

You have referenced an unknown code page or keyboard ID number, or used an invalid combination. Correct the command syntax and try again.

CONTENT OF DESTINATION LOST BEFORE COPY

You have invoked the COPY command to combine files, but the syntax caused the destination file to be overwritten before the combining process could complete. Restore the lost files from backup, correct the syntax, and try again.

CONVERT LOST CHAINS TO FILES?

CHKDSK has discovered lost chains, which are areas of the disk that include data not assigned to files in the FAT. Answer Y to this question if you would like to recover this disk space. CHKDSK will convert the lost chains to files, giving them the name FILE*nnnn*.CHK, where *nnnn* is a number from 0000 to 9999. You can review, edit, rename, or delete these files as you wish.

CURRENT DRIVE IS NO LONGER VALID

The currently logged drive does not have a disk in it, the drive door is open, or the drive is unrecognizable on a network. Change to another drive with a disk in it. Insert a disk in the drive. Close the drive door.

DATA ERROR

DOS has detected inconsistencies in data while reading or writing a file. You are prompted to Abort or Retry the operation. Press R (Retry) a few times, but if the message persists, press A (Abort). Check the disk using the CHKDSK command. Make fresh backups of the data (do not overwrite current backups) and reformat the disk.

If the problem persists or occurs on several disks, have the drive serviced.

DEVICE OR CODEPAGE MISSING

DOS could not find the requested code page definition, or it has been overwritten in memory. Correct the code page parameter, if necessary. Re-invoke the MODE command for all desired code pages.

DIRECTORY ALREADY EXISTS

You have attempted to create a directory using the MD or MKDIR commands, but a directory of the same name is already on your system. Use a different name or another nesting level.

DRIVE OR DISKETTE TYPES NOT COMPATIBLE

You have attempted to use the DISKCOMP or DISKCOPY commands on drives with two different format types. Use the FC or XCOPY commands instead.

DISKETTE BAD OR INCOMPATIBLE

The diskette you are using has an incorrect format, is copy-protected, or contains data errors. If the disk is not copy-protected, use the CHKDSK command to attempt to correct the problems.

DUPLICATE FILE NAME

You have attempted to rename a file to the name of an existing file or directory. Use a different name.

DUPLICATE REDIRECTION

You have used the redirection symbols to read data from a file being written to. Revise the syntax using a unique output file name.

ERROR IN EXE FILE

The application's executable file contains errors that interfere with processing. The file may be incompatible with your current version of DOS. Check for the correct DOS version; if the version is correct, copy a new executable file from backup copies or the master disk. If the problem persists, discard the executable files.

ERROR LOADING OPERATING SYSTEM

The operating system files cannot be found or have become corrupted. Use the SYS command to copy the system files to the drive and copy the CONFIG.SYS and AUTOEXEC.BAT files to the root directory if necessary. If you cannot restore the system files, boot from a floppy disk, back up your data, and reformat the disk using the FORMAT /S command.

ERROR READING DIRECTORY

The file allocation table or subdirectory structure has become corrupted. Back up whatever data you can on blank diskettes; do not overwrite previous backups. Reformat the disk. If the problem persists, have the drive serviced.

ERROR READING SYSTEM FILE

One of the operating system files has become corrupted. Back up your data, if possible. Restart your system. If you cannot restart, reinstall the operating system. If the problem persists, have your hardware serviced.

ERROR READING (OR WRITING) TO DEVICE

The peripheral device could not accept data being sent to it, or DOS was unable to process data sent from the device. Check that the device is on line, that the baud rate at which you are sending data is not too fast, and that the data being sent is appropriate for the device; for example, do not send data at 9600 baud if the device can only process 1200 baud, and do not send binary files to a device that can accept only ASCII files.

ERROR READING (OR WRITING) DRIVE

This message usually indicates a corrupted disk in the drive. Try another disk; if the problem persists, try rebooting the system. If the problem continues, have the drive serviced.

ERROR READING PARTITION TABLE

The hard disk's partition table is unusable. Use FDISK to set up the partition table before attempting to format the disk. If this problem persists, have the drive serviced.

EXEC FAILURE

The application's executable file contains errors that interfere with processing, or the file cannot be opened because too many files are already open. The file may be incompatible with your current version of DOS. Check for the correct DOS version. If the DOS version is correct, copy a new executable file from backup copies or the master disk. Increase the number of open files by editing the FILES command in CONFIG.SYS, and rebooting the computer. If you determine that the executable file is damaged, discard it.

EXPANDED MEMORY MANAGER NOT PRESENT

You must install the expanded memory manager before installing drivers that require this memory. Move the expanded memory manager initialization line to an earlier position in the CONFIG.SYS file.

EXPANDED MEMORY STATUS SHOWS ERROR

The driver has detected an error in your expanded memory manager. Consult the documentation for your expanded memory manager to solve the problem.

EXTENDED MEMORY MANAGER NOT PRESENT

You must install the XMS extended memory manager HIMEM.SYS before installing drivers that require this memory, such as EMM386.EXE. Move the HIMEM.SYS initialization line to an earlier position in the CONFIG.SYS file.

FAIL ON INT 24

DOS has encountered a unrecoverable critical error during processing; for example, a mechanical drive failure or corrupted file. If the computer has stopped altogether, try to restart. If you can replicate the problem, delete the files that cause the problem, or have the part serviced.

FCB UNAVAILABLE

DOS has been instructed to access a file control block that is out of range. Edit the FCBS command in CONFIG.SYS. If the problem persists, contact technical support for the application in use when you saw this message.

FILE ALLOCATION TABLE BAD

The file allocation table has become corrupted. Back up whatever data that you can on blank diskettes. Do not overwrite previous backups. You may solve the problem by invoking the CHKDSK command. If necessary, reformat the disk. If the problem persists, have the drive serviced.

FILE CANNOT BE COPIED ONTO ITSELF

You have specified the same file as both the source and target. This often happens when wildcard characters have not been used carefully. Change the file specification for the source or target as necessary, and try again.

FILE CREATION ERROR

One of the following has happened:

- There was not enough space on the disk or chosen sub-directory for the file you tried to create.

- The file you tried to create already exists and is read-only.

- You tried to rename a file using a file name that already exists.

- You attempted to redirect output to an invalid filename. Refer to *Part One* for details on valid names for files.

If the file is on the root directory, check that the maximum number of root directory files (512) has not been reached. If the root directory (or entire disk) is full, delete some other files and try again. If the file in question is read-only, use a different target name, a different directory location, or use the ATTRIB command to remove the read-only attribute. You may be attempting to overwrite a hidden file; try a different target name or location. Also, if you are renaming files, use a different target name or location.

FILE IS CROSS-LINKED

CHKDSK has found two files that share the same area of the disk. If you have specified the /F option, the named file is truncated to remove the discrepancy.

FILE NOT FOUND

The requested file was not found on the currently logged directory or any of the directories specified with the PATH or APPEND commands. This message will also appear if the specified subdirectory is empty. Check the file name for correct spelling and correct location. If necessary, change the search path.

FOR CANNOT BE NESTED

You have attempted to use the FOR command within another FOR command in a batch file. Edit the batch file, using only one FOR command per line.

GENERAL FAILURE

The disk in the drive was not formatted or was formatted for a system other than DOS. Reformat the disk. If the problem continues, have the drive serviced.

I/O ERROR

DOS has discovered a RAM error while processing. Check the status of all memory-resident applications for conflicts with the current application. If necessary, have the computer serviced.

INCOMPATIBLE SWITCHES

You have used mutually-exclusive options on the command line. Review the syntax and enter the correct options.

INCORRECT DOS VERSION

You entered a DOS external command for a version that is different from the DOS version currently in RAM. Reboot with the correct version of DOS, or use the correct executable file for the command.

INCORRECT NUMBER OF PARAMETERS

See the "Invalid parameter" error message entry.

INSUFFICIENT DISK SPACE

You have used up all the available space on your disk for copying or creating files. Run CHKDSK to reclaim space that may be occupied by lost clusters. If necessary, delete some files.

INSUFFICIENT MEMORY

You do not have sufficient RAM to process the command you entered. Remove some memory-resident files. Reboot the computer if necessary. Add more RAM to your system to accommodate the application or command.

INTERMEDIATE FILE ERROR DURING PIPE

A temporary file, created during a piping operation, has become corrupted. The disk may be too full, too many files may be open, or a hardware problem has prevented successful processing. Run CHKDSK to determine if problems exist on the data drive. Delete unnecessary files to make room on the disk. Make sure the disk is not write-protected. If too many files were open, change the FILES command in CONFIG.SYS and reboot the computer.

INTERNAL ERROR

A memory conflict or other technical error has occurred. Reboot the computer. If you detect a pattern to the appearance of the error, re-store the problem application or DOS file from backup or re-install the file from master disks and try it again. If the message appears randomly, have the computer serviced by a qualified technician. Do not overwrite current backups with new backups after seeing this message until the cause is determined and the problem solved.

INVALID ALLOCATION UNIT

The file allocation table is indicating an invalid disk location for a file. If you specified the /F parameter, the file size is changed to zero bytes and the data is lost.

INVALID CODE PAGE

You have referenced an unknown code page number. Correct the command syntax and try again. Refer to the NLSFUNC and MODE commands in *Part Four*, as well as the COUNTRY command in *Appendix A*, for details regarding code pages.

INVALID COMMAND.COM

See the "Bad or missing command interpreter" error message entry.

INVALID DATE

DOS cannot recognize the date format you have entered, or you have entered a non-existent date. Check your entry and try again.

INVALID DIRECTORY

You have entered an invalid directory name or the name of a directory that does not exist, or DOS has discovered an invalid directory on the disk. Check the spelling of the directory name and re-enter it if it is incorrect. If the invalid directory was discovered by DOS, back up what files you can onto fresh backup disks. Do not overwrite current backups. Reformat or replace the disk.

INVALID DISK CHANGE

DOS has discovered that you have changed disks during processing. Return the original disk to the drive. If disks have not been changed, this message may signal a hardware problem; have the drive serviced.

INVALID DRIVE SPECIFICATION

You have entered the letter of a drive that does not exist. Enter a different drive letter or assign the drive letter using the ASSIGN or SUBST command.

INVALID DEVICE REQUEST

DOS was unable to process a device driver command. Check the configuration syntax for the driver file and try again. If the syntax is correct, this message may indicate a corrupted device driver file or hardware failure. Recopy the driver file and try again. If necessary, have your system serviced.

INVALID DRIVE IN SEARCH PATH

You have referenced a drive letter in the PATH command that is out of range on your system. Edit the PATH command syntax or the LASTDRIVE command in CONFIG.SYS.

INVALID FILENAME

You have entered a file name containing invalid or wildcard characters, or you have used a reserved device name as a file name. Try the command again using a different file specification.

INVALID FUNCTION PARAMETER

See the "Invalid parameter" error message entry.

INVALID HANDLE

An application has attempted to access a file handle that is out of range. Contact technical support for the application that was running when you received this message.

INVALID KEYWORD

See the "Invalid parameter" error message entry.

INVALID MEMORY BLOCK ADDRESS

See the "Bad UMB Number" error message entry.

INVALID PARAMETER

You have not specified the correct option switches on the command line, or have duplicated parameters, or have combined parameters illegally. Review the correct syntax of the command and try it again.

INVALID PARAMETER COMBINATION

See the "Invalid parameter" error message entry.

INVALID PARTITION TABLE

DOS has detected an error in the fixed disk's partition information. Back up whatever data you can and run FDISK to initialize a valid partition table.

INVALID PATH

You invoked the RD or RMDIR commands using the name of the currently logged directory. Log onto the parent directory and try again. You cannot remove the root directory.

You have specified a nonexistent directory, or one that DOS cannot find. Check the drive and path specification, the spelling of the directory name, and the settings of the PATH and APPEND commands.

INVALID PATH, NOT DIRECTORY, OR DIRECTORY NOT EMPTY

DOS is not able to locate the specified directory, or you entered a file in place of a directory name, or the directory contains files (or other nested subdirectories) and cannot be removed. Check the spelling of the directory name or list the contents of the directory. If it appears empty, it may contain hidden files. Use the DIR /A:H command to reveal any possibly hidden files.

INVALID SWITCH

See the "Invalid parameter" error message entry.

INVALID SYNTAX

DOS could not process the syntax you entered. Review the correct command syntax and try again.

INVALID TIME

DOS cannot recognize the time format you have entered. Check your entry and try again.

INVALID VOLUME ID

You have entered an invalid volume ID string. Refer to the LABEL command in *Part Four* for information regarding valid volume labels.

MEMORY ALLOCATION ERROR

DOS was not able to configure RAM properly. Reboot the computer. If the problem does not go away, reboot from a floppy disk and use the SYS command to copy new system files onto your hard disk. If the problem persists, have your computer's memory boards serviced.

MUST SPECIFY ON OR OFF

You have entered an invalid parameter for a command that requires either an ON or OFF parameter. Correct the syntax and re-enter the command.

NLSFUNC NOT INSTALLED

You have attempted to reference code pages for international character sets prior to invoking the NLSFUNC command. Invoke NLSFUNC and try again. Refer to the NLSFUNC and MODE commands in *Part Four*, and the COUNTRY command in *Appendix A*, for more information on installing code pages.

NO EXTENDED MEMORY AVAILABLE

The XMS extended memory has been allocated to other applications and resident functions. Deactivate other drivers to make room for your RAM disk.

NO FIXED DISKS PRESENT

DOS was not able to detect the presence of a fixed disk drive. Check your computer's setup parameters for the correct drive type. If necessary, perform a low-level format and repartition the disk drive. If you cannot solve the problem yourself, have the computer serviced by a competent technician.

NO ROOM IN DIRECTORY

You have exceeded the limit on the number of allowable files in your root directory (512 files). Copy the file to a subdirectory or different disk.

NON-SYSTEM DISK OR DISK ERROR

DOS cannot find system files on the current disk. Insert a disk containing system files or boot from the hard disk if it contains system files.

NOT ENOUGH MEMORY

See the "Insufficient memory" error message entry.

OUT OF ENVIRONMENT SPACE

You have initialized too many operating system variables. Remove some variables using the SET command or increase the size of the environment using the SHELL command in CONFIG.SYS, and reboot the computer.

PARAMETER FORMAT NOT CORRECT

See the "Invalid parameter" error message entry.

PARAMETER VALUE NOT ALLOWED

See the "Invalid parameter" error message entry.

PARAMETER VALUE NOT IN ALLOWED RANGE

See the "Invalid parameter" error message entry.

PARAMETERS NOT COMPATIBLE

See the "Invalid parameter" error message entry.

PARSE ERROR

You have entered a syntax error, but DOS cannot locate COM-MAND.COM to display a more precise error message. Reboot the computer if necessary; check the command syntax and try again.

PATH NOT FOUND

See the "Invalid path" error message entry.

PRINTER ERROR

DOS cannot send data to your printing device. Make sure the device is on-line, has paper ready, and that the output has not been redirected to a different port.

PROGRAM TOO BIG TO FIT IN MEMORY

See the "Insufficient memory" error message entry.

READ FAULT ERROR

DOS cannot read data on the disk. Re-insert the disk in the drive and press R (Retry). If the error persists, run CHKDSK on the disk; if the disk is unrecoverable, reformat or discard it.

REQUIRED FONT NOT LOADED

DISPLAY.SYS has not been initialized to include the desired font. Edit CONFIG.SYS, increasing the number of subfonts, and reboot the computer.

REQUIRED PARAMETER MISSING

See the "Invalid parameter" error message entry.

SAME PARAMETER ENTERED TWICE

See the "Invalid parameter" error message entry.

SECTOR NOT FOUND

DOS has discovered a formatting error on the disk. If DOS allows it, back up the file being accessed at the time this message appeared to recover whatever portion may still be usable. Run CHKDSK to try to solve the disk's problems. If the problem persists, reformat or discard the disk.

SEEK ERROR

See the "Read fault error" error message entry.

SHARING VIOLATION

You have attempted to reopen or write to a file that is already open. This often occurs on a network, but may also occur on single-user systems with SHARE installed. Use your current application's commands to close the data file before attempting to reopen or write new data to it.

SOURCE DOES NOT CONTAIN BACKUP FILES

DOS was unable to locate the files CONTROL.001 and BACK-UP.001 on the floppy disk. Check the disk and try again.

SPECIFIED COMMAND
SEARCH DIRECTORY BAD

The SHELL command in CONFIG.SYS contains invalid information. Edit this line in the CONFIG.SYS file and reboot the computer.

SPECIFIED DRIVE DOES NOT EXIST, OR IS NON-REMOVABLE

You have invoked a command intended for use on floppy drives, referencing a hard disk drive letter or drive letter that does not exist. Correct the syntax and try again.

SYNTAX ERROR

See the "Invalid parameter" error message entry.

TOO MANY FILES OPEN

See the "Too many open files" error message entry.

TOO MANY OPEN FILES

You have exceeded the maximum number of allowed open files on your system. Increase the maximum with the FILES command in CONFIG.SYS and reboot the computer.

TOO MANY PARAMETERS

See the "Invalid parameter" error message entry.

TOO MANY REDIRECTIONS

You have redirected data output to a device that does not exist or have attempted to redirect data that has already been redirected. Correct the command line syntax for the correct device or a single redirection and try again.

TOP LEVEL PROCESS ABORTED, CANNOT CONTINUE

DOS was unable to return to the parent routine after completing a nested subroutine. Reboot the computer. Recopy the application files from backup or master disks. If using a batch file, edit the syntax for nested subroutines.

TRACK 0 BAD

DOS has detected disk errors in a critical portion of the disk. Reboot the computer and try accessing the disk again. If the problem persists, discard the disk. If the problem occurs for an inordinate number of disks, have your floppy drive serviced.

UNABLE TO CREATE DIRECTORY

You have attempted to create a directory using the MD or MKDIR commands, but either a directory of the same name is already on your system, you have reached the limit on the number of entries in your root directory, or your disk is write-protected. Use a different name or try to create the directory at another nesting level.

UNRECOGNIZED COMMAND IN CONFIG.SYS

DOS could not recognize a command in the CONFIG.SYS file when booting. Other messages that appear before this one may help you determine which lines are invalid. Edit CONFIG.SYS and correct the invalid lines. If you are editing CONFIG.SYS with a word processor, be sure that you save the file as an ASCII file.

UNRECOGNIZED SWITCH

See the "Invalid parameter" error message entry.

UNRECOVERABLE READ OR WRITE ERROR

DOS could not read or write data to the disk. The disk is probably damaged. Use a different disk to save the current data. Run CHKDSK on the damaged disk to attempt to recover what files you can. Reformat or discard the bad disk.

WARNING! INVALID PARAMETER IGNORED

DOS cannot recognize a parameter you have entered on the HIMEM initialization line in CONFIG.SYS. Edit this line in the CONFIG.SYS file and reboot the computer.

WARNING! NO FILES WERE FOUND TO RESTORE

Your file specification did not match files on the backup floppy disk. Log onto the target subdirectory before invoking the command. Review the command syntax carefully, and re-enter the command with the correct file path specification for the hard disk. Refer to the RESTORE command in *Part Four* for detailed syntax information.

WRITE FAULT ERROR

DOS cannot write data to the disk. Re-insert the disk in the drive, and press R (Retry). If the error persists, run CHKDSK on the disk; if the disk is unrecoverable, discard it.

WRITE PROTECT ERROR

DOS cannot write data to the disk because it is write-protected. Remove the write-protection tab from the disk, re-insert the disk in the drive, and press R (Retry). If the error persists, use a different disk.

Index

Note: This index shows primary explanations of important topics in **boldface** type. References to illustrations appear in *italic* type.

D

T

Help Yourself with Another Quality Sybex Book

Understanding 1-2-3 Release 2.3 & 2.4 for DOS

Rebecca Bridges Altman

This practical introduction offers hands-on coverage of everything from start-up to advanced techniques. Learn to plan, build, and use business spreadsheets; design informative spreadsheet reports; translate the numbers into dazzling presentation graphics; and much more. Covers version 2.3, plus all of 2.4's new features, including BackSolver and SmartIcons.

715pp; 7 1/2" x 9"
ISBN: 0-7821-1133-5

Available at Better Bookstores Everywhere

Help Yourself with Another Quality Sybex Book

Help Yourself with Another Quality Sybex Book

Mastering Windows 3.1
Robert Cowart

The complete guide to installing, using, and making the most of Windows on IBM PCs and compatibles now in an up-to-date new edition. Part I provides detailed, hands-on coverage of major Windows features that are essential for day-to-day use. Part II offers complete tutorials on the accessory programs. Part III explores a selection of advanced topics.

600pp; 7 1/2" x 9"
ISBN: 0-89588-842-4

Available
at Better
Bookstores
Everywhere

Sybex. Help Yourself.

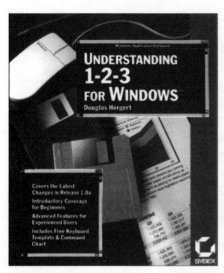

Help Yourself with
Another Quality Sybex Book

DOS Commands by Function

Function	Command to Use
Perform commands conditionally	IF
Place comments in system or batch files	REM
Print a file from DOS	PRINT
Protect files on a network	SHARE
Protect the system from viruses	VSAFE
Prolong battery life	POWER
Recover an accidentally erased file	UNDELETE
Recover from an accidental disk format	MIRROR, UNFORMAT
Redirect parallel output to serial	MODE
Remove a computer virus	MSAV
Remove an empty subdirectory	RD, RMDIR
Repeat commands in a batch file	FOR, GOTO
Restore data from backups	COPY, REPLACE, RESTORE, XCOPY
Return from a secondary processor	EXIT
Run a subroutine in a batch file	CALL
Send graphics characters to the printer	GRAPHICS
Send screen output to a remote terminal	CTTY
Set a new screen length or width	MODE
Set the time	TIME
Shift the screen display right or left	MODE
Skip lines in a batch file	GOTO
Sort data	SORT
Speed up the system	DEFRAG, FAST-OPEN, SMARTDRV
Speed up or slow down key response	MODE
Stop the screen from scrolling	Ctrl-S, MORE
Suppress batch file line display	ECHO OFF
Suspend batch file processing	PAUSE